DOWN AT THE DEPOT

Other Books by Edwin P. Alexander

THE COLLECTOR'S BOOK OF THE LOCOMOTIVE

IRON HORSES

AMERICAN LOCOMOTIVES

MODEL RAILROADS

THE PENNSYLVANIA RAILROAD, A PICTORIAL HISTORY

Edwin P. Alexander

DOWN AT THE DEPOT

American Railroad Stations
from 1831 to 1920

Clarkson N. Potter, Inc./Publisher   NEW YORK

DISTRIBUTED BY CROWN PUBLISHERS, INC.

Another One for Maggy

Contents

Preface

*T*HIS ALBUM DEPICTS BUT A FEW OF THE TENS OF THOUSANDS OF STATIONS
as they were during the railroad era—a sampling of the then important focal points
of towns and cities across the continent. Their association with that nostalgic period,
their picturesqueness, and their distinct and often unique architecture make them
a most important part of the American past. But like the iron horses which came
to them, they are in turn becoming just as antiquated in terms of modern transport.

The trend is already quite definite. Only in densely populated areas where mass
transportation is planned can such structures for railroad patrons be economically
justified. So, perhaps sadly to those historically or nostalgically minded, these buildings are disappearing.

The purpose here is to recapture an important part of the railroad era—to show
railroad stations when they looked their best, were busiest, or were architecturally
outstanding. Of course, many of the smaller buildings illustrated make no pretense
of being representative of the last, but this should be compensated for by trains,
people, or conveyances frequently shown.

Sometimes, dates and data have been scant or unavailable, and in a few cases an
estimation has been made. Most of the pictures are from the author's collection,
but the much appreciated cooperation of many railroads has been outstanding. Due
credit has been accorded all pictures from these and individual sources, wherever
known. In a number of instances, a picture of a train or locomotive appears opposite that of a station. This equipment would be generally typical of the type
which passed through the station at some period of its history.

So, indulge in a bit of remembrance of the wonderful days of the "Limiteds,"
the "Expresses," the "Specials," and the "Flyers" as you look at these pictures.
And by no means forget the people associated with them, station agent and train
crew, baggageman and engineer—all are in the memories to be summoned up.

BORDENTOWN, NEW JERSEY Camden and Amboy

In the early 1830s, as at many other stopping places on the first railroads, an inn served as a station. This was the Delaware River Terminal of New Jersey's first railroad at Bordentown.

Introduction

*I*N THE EARLY DAYS OF RAIL TRAVEL THERE WERE NO STATIONS; THE PRIMARY concern of railroad builders was to get the rails laid and the trains running. So the new mode of transportation followed the methods of the stage and canal companies, neither of which had provided special buildings to take care of passengers or freight. Hotels or inns were the departure and terminal points for travelers. Tickets, except in a few cases when the conductor or captain collected the money from the passengers, were sold at the departure points or at business places in the towns served.

Some pioneer railroads provided ticket booths but no accommodations for passengers. Even the earliest Baltimore & Ohio structure, Mount Clare in Baltimore, was at first only a booking or ticket office; no shelter or other facilities being available. In some cases houses were adapted for use as stations until such could be constructed.

Trains in those early times departed from a street or other location in town, and the following are excerpts from old advertising:

". . . starts every morning from the corner of Broad and Race Street—Pioneer Fast Line to Pittsburgh, Through in 3½ days" [1837].

"A through train for the accommodation of Western Passengers will leave the vicinity of Broad & Callowhill Street. A. McHaffey Supt. Columbia & Philadelphia Rail Road." [1837].

". . . Departure from State Street, Albany." Mohawk & Hudson (1834).

"Summer Arrangement—Up trains will leave City Hall for . . ." New York & Harlem (1847) (Small broadside. Late for a "no station" ad.)

Later, of course, Mount Clare (p. 11) became a "station." The second Baltimore & Ohio depot was built in 1831 at Frederick, Maryland (p. 51). The B. & O. is thus credited with the first two substantially built structures to be called stations in the United States.

Because the railroads emanated from the larger cities in their formative years, the early station buildings were constructed there. But it was not until ten to fifteen years after their primitive beginnings that the term "architecture" could really be applied to them. In the larger towns and cities brick buildings with wooden train sheds were the order, and frequently the latter were destroyed by fire caused by locomotives' sparks.

By the 1840s stations really worthy of note were being built. The unique station at New Haven, Connecticut, designed by Henry Austin and completed in 1849 (p. 252), was most outstanding. It was a combination of many styles—Italian, Indian, and Chinese—and the first American station with a campanile.

Providence's first Union station was built in 1848—the work of Thomas Tefft at age twenty-two! It was the first built in the Romanesque manner, and as late as 1885, it was voted one of the twenty best buildings in the United States, an unusual tribute considering it was thirty-seven years old at the time (p. 283).

The Salem station by Gridley J. F. Bryant, completed in 1847, was again different in design—medieval in appearance and Norman in concept. It was, as Carroll Meeks said, "regrettable that this venerable station could not be preserved from demolition as a memorial to early American industry" (p. 142).

Through the 1850s the railroads serving such cities as Philadelphia, New York, Harrisburg, Baltimore, and Troy erected a number of substantial stations, and this trend became well established for years. By the 1870s the eastern half of the country had a large number of such buildings in a variety of architectural forms from Gothic and Romanesque to Italian villa or "Railroad style."

Comparatively few smaller stations were architecturally designed. Generally most were planned by the railroads' engineering departments at headquarters and built under their supervision by their carpenters and engineers. Some might even have been called prefabricated such as the one at Ladson, South Carolina (p. 66).

A standard design provided little chance for individuality, and stations by the hundreds, even thousands, were just utilitarian buildings. Fortunately, many other thousands were distinctive in some form or other, and their picturesqueness stimulates today's nostalgia.

It took some years for the railroads in the western territories and states to catch up with the East. As with the early eastern lines, the idea was to get the rails down and trains operating; other things like stations could come later. Similarly, ticket offices often came before stations, as in Kansas City (p. 12).

Most of the first western stations were quite primitive and makeshift. Often old cars (p. 13, Lariat, Colorado) were used "temporarily," which might have meant for years. As late as the early 1870s, Indians were burning isolated stations. Even the larger depots were nothing to write home about until about the 1890s, but from that time on, their architectural design kept pace with the East.

Typical scenes at country stations in the 1880s.

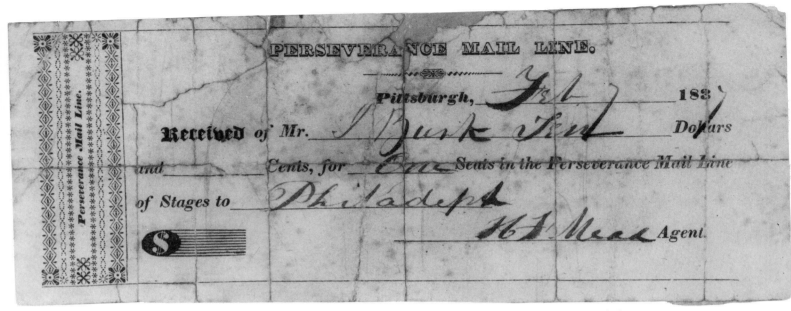

A ticket dated 1837 on the Perseverance Stage Line, later superceded by the Pennsylvania State System of Railroads.

KANSAS CITY, MISSOURI (1870s)   Missouri Pacific

The first ticket office in Kansas City was in this building—located nowhere near the tracks.

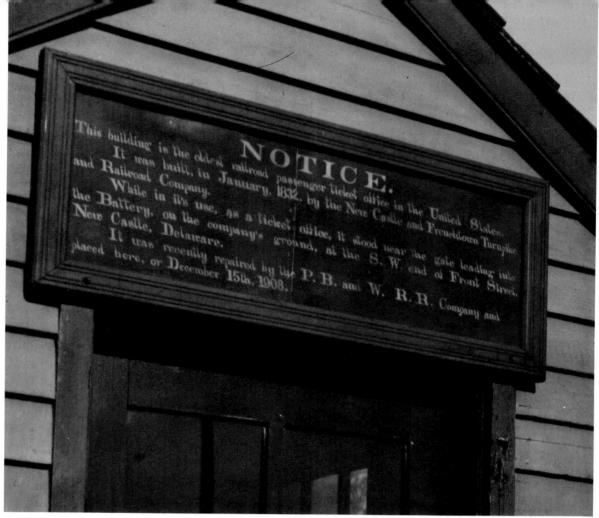

This ticket office was the first building of the Newcastle-Frenchtown Railroad (later the Pennsylvania Railroad) for passenger accommodation. Used many years later by crossing watchmen, it was subsequently rescued, and is now preserved at Newcastle, Delaware.

LARIAT, COLORADO   Denver and Rio Grande

Just as in the East many years before, the expanding western railroads used makeshift ticket offices such as this one at Lariat, Colorado.

PART I

The Country Stations

SINCE THEY WERE FIRST BUILT, COUNTRY STATIONS OR DEPOTS WERE THE FOCAL point of most communities. They were a kind of social center, the source of local news and gossip. No one arriving or departing, stranger or resident, went unnoticed, and farewells and welcomes were sincere—not only between relatives but between strangers and townsfolk. In the days of the horse and buggy, the station was the only means of intercourse with the outside world.

Train time was an event at the depot for, besides travelers, it brought news, mail, and merchandise. Grown-ups came by foot, carriage, wagon, or perhaps trolley. Boys knew the engines and the engineers, to whose profession they most aspired. Watches were set by the station clock, although legend says it was by the locomotive's whistle. Telegrams, before the ubiquitous telephone, were dispatched and received at the depot. It was a scene of continuous activity, even at other than train time.

Employees and train crews were, of course, the essential elements in the picture. At the smallest, one-man depot, the station agent took care of everything— selling tickets, handling baggage, keeping the stove going, and doing dozens of necessary jobs. Usually, he was the telegraph operator, too, handling train orders as well as public telegrams.

In the somewhat larger stations, there might have been a baggageman who also took care of express shipment. If the station was a "combination," one with space for freight, handling such shipments would also be part of his work.

The towns represented by many of these stations have grown—perhaps into cities—since these pictures were taken. But we are looking at the past.

< ADAMS, MASSACHUSETTS   Boston & Albany

In the northwest corner of Massachusetts, fifteen miles from Pittsfield, is Adams. Here about 1912 is a three-car local slowing for the station stop.

Charles Shackford.

ANCHORAGE, KENTUCKY   Louisville & Nashville

No. 8, the Birmingham-Cincinnati express carrying through cars for New York, slows to pick up the mail at Anchorage in this 1941 view. It is twelve miles from Louisville.   *L. & N.*

ANNAPOLIS JUNCTION, MARYLAND (1835)   Baltimore & Ohio

As early as 1831, while the B. & O.'s "Main Stem" was being built westward from Baltimore, it was recognized that a branch line to Washington was also necessary. Eighteen miles from Baltimore, Annapolis Junction became the branch station. The line was completed and the station opened in 1835. This picture was taken in the 1860s.

ASHLAND, WISCONSIN (1885)   Northern Pacific

This combination depot seventy-six miles from Duluth dates from 1885. It was moved from Ashland and became the South Superior station in 1892.   *N. P.*

AURORA, NEW YORK   Lehigh Valley

This is the local depot at Aurora in 1906. The engine is a 4-4-0 built at the L. V. Sayre Shops in 1885, Class E-22, No. 2578.   *L. V.*

BARNEGAT, NEW JERSEY   Central Railroad of N.J.

The Jersey Central's branch from Lakehurst ends at Barnegat, twenty-two miles away. Locomotive 756 couldn't come much closer to the bumper in this photograph taken in 1947.   *Thomas Annin.*

BASALT, COLORADO   Colorado Midland

This is a 1895 view of the Colorado Midland's depot and yards at Basalt in the heart of Colorado mining country.   *Library, State Historical Society of Colorado.*

BELDEN, CALIFORNIA   Western Pacific

Belden station deep in the Feather River Canyon was built during the construction of the railroad, and this photograph is from the 1920s. It is no longer a station stop but is used by the road's employees.   *W. P.*

BIG INDIAN, NEW YORK   Ulster & Delaware

Two trains meet at Big Indian thirty-seven miles from Kingston, and passengers and a baggageman pause for their picture in the 1880s. The engine is No. 4.

BETHLEHEM, NEW HAMPSHIRE   Boston & Maine

An old P.R.R. excursion book of 1896 says of Bethlehem in the White Mountains: "one of the most popular resorts. 10,000 people annually spend a week or longer. Bethlehem enjoys the proud distinction of being the highest village east of the Rockies. It is 1450 feet above sea level." (Actually, there are many others.)

BRISTOL, TENNESSEE   Norfolk & Western

This station is on the Tennessee-Virginia state line, 130 miles from Knoxville via Southern Railway and 403 miles from Norfolk. It was near train time in 1917 when this picture was taken.   *N. & W.*

BROCKVILLE, ONTARIO, CANADA (1860)   Canadian National

Almost midway between Montreal and Toronto is Brockville, and its neat brick station is shown as it appeared about 1870. The old high switch target is also worthy of note.   *C. N.*

BYCOT, PENNSYLVANIA (1890s)   Philadelphia & Reading

Probably the smallest stone station ever built, this little building was on the New Hope Branch of the Reading. Although in the farming area of Bucks County, some commuting to Philadelphia was done from here.

The 2-8-0 locomotive, No. 918, is typical of those that stopped at Bycot.

CAMBRIDGE, NEW YORK (1852)   Delaware & Hudson

The Delaware & Hudson's Cambridge station, shown in the 1890s, was on the Rutland & Washington Branch fifty-seven miles from Rutland. It was abandoned in 1900 and made into a dwelling.   *D. & H.*

Locomotive No. 555 and its train probably operated past Cambridge.

CANAAN, CONNECTICUT   New Haven

Once a busy junction and crossing of the New York, New Haven and Hartford, and the Central New England (which later combined), the old Canaan station looked like this about 1950. The New Haven line running north and south was the route to the Berkshires, and the Central New England's track ran from Hartford to Poughkeepsie. In 1908 sixteen trains of the New Haven stopped here, and the C.N.E. scheduled twenty.   *N. H.*

No. 258, a N. Y. N. H. & H. 2-6-0 locomotive, is shown as it appeared in 1895.

CAPE MAY, NEW JERSEY (1870s)   Pennsylvania Railroad

At the tip of New Jersey, Cape May had been a summer resort for years before
the railroad came, having been reached by steamboat. By 1868 the West Jersey

Railroad and three other lines progressively built from Camden reached Cape May
and made the seashore area much more accessible. This drawing shows a scene
shortly after the opening of the line with the station, vacationists, and the ocean.

CAPISTRANO, CALIFORNIA   Atchison, Topeka & Santa Fe
This is the old Moorish-style Capistrano station of the Santa Fe in the 1900s.

CASTLE ROCK, COLORADO   Denver & Rio Grande
A train pauses at Castle Rock about 1910. On close inspection a passenger can be seen getting aboard so the fireman was evidently busy during the stop. This station is 32.5 miles south of Denver. *Library, State Historical Society of Colorado.*

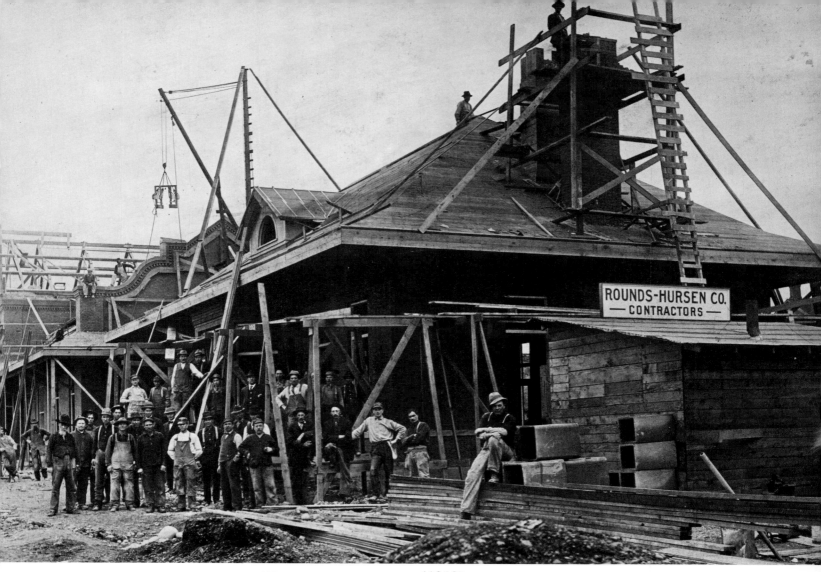

CENTRALIA, WASHINGTON (1912)   Northern Pacific

Just about midway between Seattle and Portland is Centralia. This view shows the station under construction in 1912.   *N. P.*

One of the locomotives that might have stopped here was No. 328, a 4-6-0 engine, pictured in 1907.

CHARLOTTE, NORTH CAROLINA   Southern

On the Southern's main line at Charlotte in the 1890s, two horse-drawn hotel omnibuses wait for debarking passengers from the train. The large brick station was evidently planned and built anticipating paving of the street.

Arthur Hampton Collection.

CHASKA, TENNESSEE (1900s)   Louisville & Nashville

The Chaska station was just being completed when this picture was taken—note the man on the roof. A water tank was also part of the facilities built as part of the L. & N.'s Cincinnati-Knoxville main line in the early 1900s.   *L. & N.*

CHATHAM, NEW YORK (1860s)   New York & Harlem

The New York & Harlem (later the New York Central) was completed to Chatham in 1852, and this picture was taken in the 1860s. The early flat-roofed passenger cars help date the picture.   *N.Y.C.*

>

CHAZY LAKE, NEW YORK (1892)   Delaware & Hudson

This little building is another candidate for "smallest" station. It was a stop for summer camps in the area thirty miles west of Plattsburg on the D. & H. Branch to Lake Placid. Despite its small size note that it was also a Post Office, Express Office, and Western Union Office.   *D. & H.*

No. 499, a 4-4-0 locomotive, pulls a three-car passenger train.

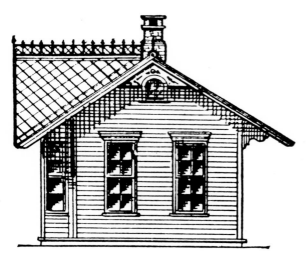

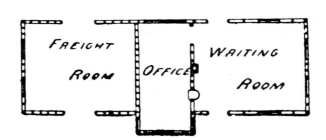

FREIGHT ROOM   OFFICE   WAITING ROOM

CHERRY FORD, PENNSYLVANIA (1880s)   Lehigh Valley

This is a fairly typical design for a small combination station of the Lehigh Valley.

The 2-8-0 locomotive, No. 597, was built in 1894.

CHESLEY, ONTARIO, CANADA   Canadian National

   Northwest of Hamilton, Ontario, by 94.6 miles is Chesley. Here in 1957 is a southbound way freight in a picture by Don Wood. The station would date to the 1900s.   *C. N.*

CHEYENNE, WYOMING (1868)   Union Pacific

   If the date of the picture can be relied upon, this was the Union Pacific's first station in Cheyenne (built 1868, photograph c. 1880).   *U. P.*

CLINTON, TENNESSEE   Southern
    Here is Clinton, as it appeared about 1900. This station is twenty-one miles
west of Knoxville.   *C. L. Graham.*

    This freight train, which might have passed through Clinton, is being pulled by
a 2-8-0 locomotive, No. 388.   *So.*

CLINTON CORNERS, NEW YORK (1880s)   New Haven

Originally this station was on the Poughkeepsie & Eastern line which was later acquired by the Central New England and eventually became part of the New Haven. The picture was taken about 1900.   *Thomas Annin.*

38

CORNING, IOWA (1880s)   Chicago, Burlington & Quincy

Here is the Knox College Glee Club from Galesburg, Illinois, waiting for a train to take them home in the early 1900s.

Locomotive No. 380, a 4-4-0 Class A-3 engine, was manufactured by Danforth Cooke in 1870.   *C. B. & Q.*

COUNCIL BLUFFS, IOWA   Chicago & North Western
    Three miles east of Omaha, this was the C.N.W. station at Council Bluffs as it
looked in 1898.   *Library, State Historical Society of Colorado.*

COXTON, PENNSYLVANIA (C. 1870)   Lehigh Valley
This was a scene at Coxton, some miles northwest of Wilkes Barre, in the 1870s.

CRISMAN, COLORADO   Colorado Central

This station was identified as being on the Denver, Boulder & Western, but the engine is lettered "Colorado Central." The station is thirty miles west of Denver near Boulder.

Library, State Historical Society of Colorado.

CREEDE, COLORADO   Denver & Rio Grande

This was Creede at the end of a branch line on the D. & R. G. in 1892. According to the photograph identification it was also called Jimtown.

Library, State Historical Society of Colorado.

DURANGO, COLORADO Denver & Rio Grande

The Durango station about 1915 looked like this, complete with dual-gauge track and narrow-gauge locomotive and cars.

Library, State Historical Society of Colorado.

EAGLE, COLORADO Denver & Rio Grande

The time would appear to have been about 1918 when this photograph was taken at Eagle on the Denver & Rio Grande, but there is no data as to the occasion for the band. *Library, State Historical Association of Colorado.*

EPHRATA, WASHINGTON (1870s)   Great Northern

This is probably the most primitive station picture to be found. But despite its appearance as hardly more than a shelter, telegraph insulators can be seen above the side window. The signal, too, is interesting as are other details such as the boat in the wagon.   *Railroad Magazine.*

ELBERON, NEW JERSEY   Central Railroad of New Jersey

Two miles south of Long Branch station on the Jersey Central's line along the coast is Elberon, and this picture dates about 1900. After being shot in Washington, President Garfield was taken to his home here, where he died in September 1881.

Thomas Annin.

EVERGLADES, FLORIDA   Atlantic Coast Line

A small, Spanish-style station at the end of a branch line as it looked in 1930. This was at the southwest tip of the peninsula but has since been abandoned.

No. 54, a 4-4-0 locomotive, was built in 1891.   *S. C. L.*

FLEMINGTON JUNCTION, NEW JERSEY   Lehigh Valley

Fifty-one miles from New York, Flemington Junction was the railroad stop on the Lehigh Valley nearest to the county seat of Hunterdon. Years ago many trains stopped here; in 1909 there were twenty-three scheduled trains between the Junction and Flemington, 1.7 miles away, and fourteen main line trains.

The passenger train, pulled by Engine No. 2416, is shown as it appeared in 1906.

FORKS, COLORADO   Colorado & Southern

Forks was a junction on the Colorado & Southern and this is how it looked in the 1880s. Serving mining towns, one branch went to Black Hawk and Central City and the other to Idaho Springs and Georgetown.

Library, State Historical Society of Colorado

FORT EDWARD, NEW YORK (1880)   Delaware & Hudson
    Fifty-five miles north of Troy, this Fort Edward station, which stood at the junction of the branch line to Lake George, was built in 1880. It is supposed that the projecting case from the bay window is a train number indicator. The building was torn down in 1900.   *D. & H.*

FORT FRED STEELE, WYOMING (1870s)   Union Pacific

The station sign states "695½ miles to Omaha, 337½ miles to Ogden." According to later timetables the name was shortened to Fort Steele.   *U. P.*

Locomotive No. 58 and this train appeared in the movie *Union Pacific.*

FREDERICK, MARYLAND (1831)   Baltimore & Ohio

This was the second oldest and largest of early stations. It was built in time for the opening of the road to Frederick, sixty-one miles from Baltimore, on December 2, 1831.

No. 201 was a "Dutch Wagon" engine, built by R. Norris and Son in 1854.

FREEHAVEN, INDIANA (1860s)

Freehaven, Indiana, on the Lafayette & Indianapolis Railroad, was "somewhere south of Indianapolis, east of Vincennes, and west of Cincinnati" in Raintree County. It existed only in the imagination of Ross Lockridge, Jr., who used it for the 1860s setting of his book *Raintree County*. The station shown was a set for the film and was built by MGM in 1956 on the Louisville & Nashville's Lancaster Branch near Rowland Kentucky. The locomotive was the B. & O.'s William Mason which had been rented for the occasion. *L. & N.*

GARDINER, MONTANA   Northern Pacific

Gardiner is the northern gateway to Yellowstone National Park, fifty-four miles south of the Northern Pacific's main line at Livingston.

GENESEO, NEW YORK (1880s)   Erie

Geneseo is just south of the Erie's main line, about twenty-five miles from Rochester. This is an 1897 view of the station.   *Thomas Annin.*

GIBSON, TENNESSEE (1880s)   Louisville & Nashville

This is train No. 102 northbound at Gibson headed for Bowling Green in mid-afternoon on a day in the 1920s. The engine is No. 188, a K-2 Class Pacific built by the L. & N.   *L. & N.*

GLENS FALLS, NEW YORK (1870)   Delaware & Hudson

The coaches have met the train at Glens Falls, the luggage has been tied down, and as soon as the passengers have settled down, the entourage will be on their way leaving the spectators something to talk about. This building was abandoned in 1897 and sold; a freight station is now on the site.   *Railroad Magazine.*

GRAFTON, WEST VIRGINIA (1850s)   Baltimore & Ohio

Built in the 1850s, Grafton station and hotel was at a junction point on the main line. A Cincinnati *Enquirer* correspondent's report in 1857 says in part, "the edifice is a grand structure of the Gothic and Corinthian style of architecture and in the point of extent and dimensions and beauty of its appearance will compare favorably with many hotels in larger cities . . . parlors gorgeously furnished . . . bedrooms acme of comfort . . . scenery grand and sublime . . . one of *the* institutions of the country."

GREEN RIVER, WYOMING (1868)   Union Pacific

An early picture when the Green River station was new. Note the skyline and Desert House restaurant and especially the unusual ball signal in the right foreground. A ball is hanging below, but it is not known whether it could have been illuminated and if there was red and green glass in the housing.   *U. P.*

Locomotive No. 527 was a 4-4-0 engine.

HANOVER JUNCTION, PENNSYLVANIA (1850s)   Pennsylvania Railroad

On November 18, 1863, the special train taking President Lincoln to Gettysburg paused at Hanover Junction on the Northern Central, and these pictures were taken there. The tall figure with the stovepipe hat to the right of the locomotive is supposedly Lincoln although there is some debate about this. The train is standing on the branch from Gettysburg and would have to be turned—rails of the wye can be seen beyond the second car. The picture was taken from the roof of a car on the middle track.   *Association of American Railroads.*

A number of passengers from the special, and several of the military are evident. The fact that they, together with several ladies and photographers, would be at this rather unimportant stop seems to remove any doubt that it was the Lincoln special.

The National Archives.

HAVERSTRAW, NEW YORK (1880s)   New York, Ontario & Western

The Haverstraw depot is another good example of the station-hotel-dining-room combination of the 1860s through 1880s. The sign advertises "Hotel & Lunch Room" and "National Telegraph Office." The locomotive is N.Y.O. & W. No. 39; note the back-up headlight on its tender.   *Railroad Magazine.*

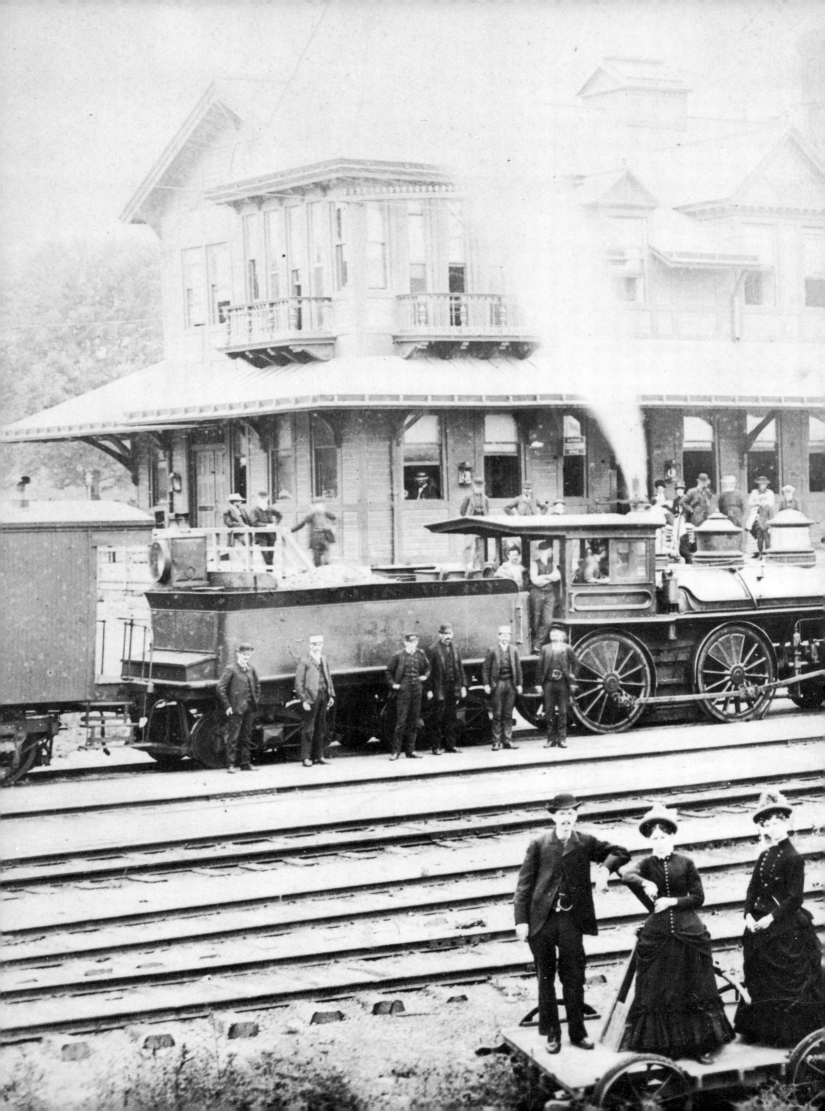

HUSTED, COLORADO   Denver & Rio Grande

    Posing for the photograph about 1909 are the station agent at Husted and the crew with engine No. 530.   *Library, State Historical Society of Colorado.*

‹

HONESDALE, PENNSYLVANIA (1875)   Delaware & Hudson

    For years people came to Honesdale to ride the "Gravity Railroad," and these views were taken in 1898. The station served its passengers on the second floor and freight on the ground level. Across the canal in the lower photograph, where a boat is waiting for its load of coal from the four-wheel "dinkies," may be seen a loaded passenger train ready to be drawn up the inclined plane (visible in the first picture to the left of the station). "The sensations of the return ride . . . are no less novel than those going in the opposite direction. Every moment brings a new surprise until the base of the incline is reached," says an advertising brochure of the times.   *D. & H.*

KENT, CONNECTICUT (1872)   New Haven

On the New Haven's line to the Berkshires, Kent is about ninety miles north of New York. Some fifty years ago, ten trains a day stopped here, and as late as the 1930s there were eight, six of which had buffet, parlor, and dining cars. The best-known train was the Berkshire Express, whose running time to or from New York was three hours.   *N. H.*

No. 127 was photographed at New Haven in 1892.

KINGSTON, NEW YORK   New York Central

This is a 1900s view of Kingston station on the New York Central's West Shore line ninety miles north of New York.

LADSON, SOUTH CAROLINA (1880s)   Southern

A Southern Railway predecessor, the South Carolina Railway built this little station with graceful curves and ornate trimmings and a freight shed in the 1880s. Actually, it was constructed at Summerville, South Carolina, and later moved on flatcars to Ladson. It was dismantled in 1935.   *So.*

LAKE GEORGE, NEW YORK (1882)   Delaware & Hudson

This picturesque branch line terminal built at Lake George in 1882, was fourteen miles from the main line junction at Fort Edward. The style is difficult to define; perhaps the "gingerbread" suggests oriental. It stood until 1911 when it was torn down and a new station built on its site the following year. *Railroad Magazine*.

The "Commodore Vanderbilt," a 4-4-0 locomotive, was designed by Walter McQueen and built in 1866.   *D. & H.*

LAMBERTVILLE, NEW JERSEY   Pennsylvania Railroad

The Belvidere Delaware Railroad started construction north along the Delaware River in 1851, and the first sixteen miles to Lambertville were opened that year. An old stone house, probably fifty years old then, was taken over to serve as a station, and was used a number of years until a larger stone building was erected. The "Bel-Del," as part of the United Railroads of New Jersey, was acquired by the Pennsylvania in 1871.

Locomotive No. 3011 (Pennsylvania R.R. numbering) was a 4-4-0 engine built at Lambertville in the 1860s.

LAMOURE, NORTH DAKOTA (1883)   Northern Pacific

Eighty-eight miles southwest of Fargo, this was Lamoure in 1883. When the depot was built, it was in Dakota Territory.   *N. P.*

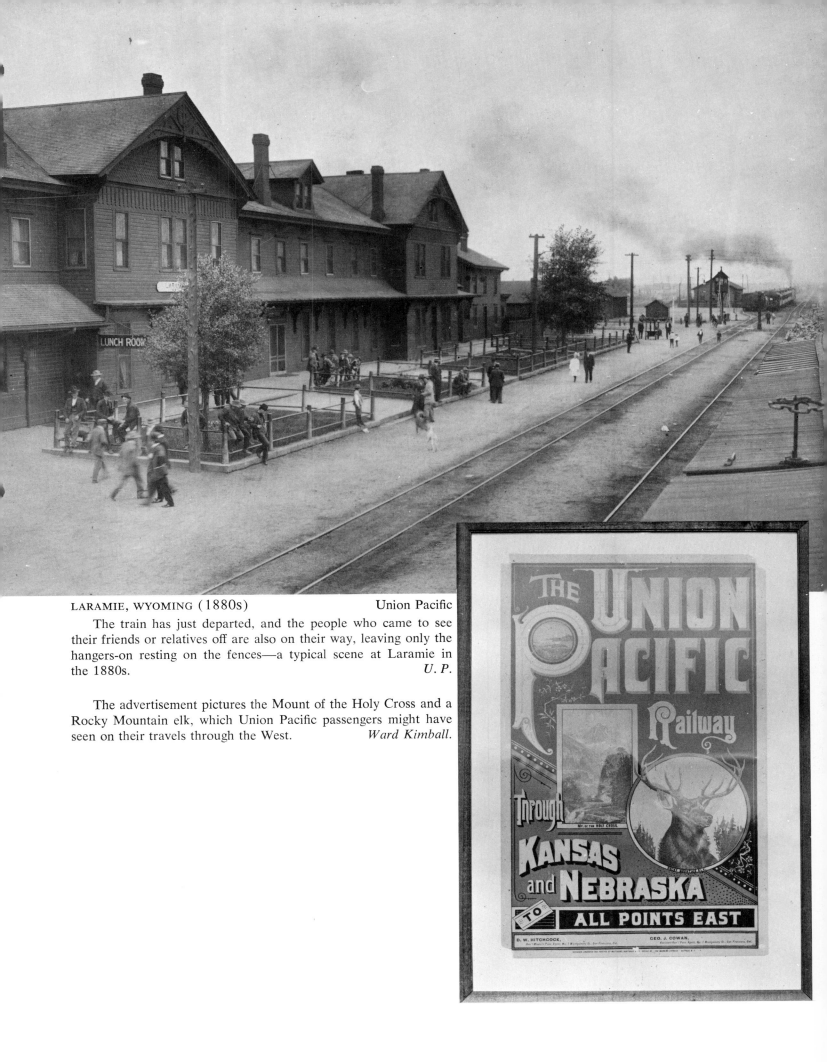

LARAMIE, WYOMING (1880s)   Union Pacific

The train has just departed, and the people who came to see
their friends or relatives off are also on their way, leaving only the
hangers-on resting on the fences—a typical scene at Laramie in
the 1880s.   *U. P.*

The advertisement pictures the Mount of the Holy Cross and a
Rocky Mountain elk, which Union Pacific passengers might have
seen on their travels through the West.   *Ward Kimball.*

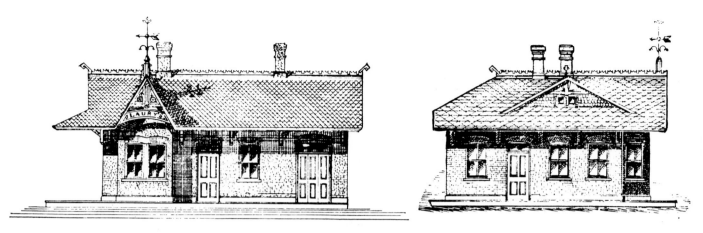

LAURY'S, PENNSYLVANIA (1880s)   Lehigh Valley

From Lehigh Valley Summer Tours, 1904: "This name has a pleasant local significance—a cozy hotel is nestled among the trees and upon an island in the (Lehigh) river, beneath the verdure, the picnics of the valley are held all through the summer."

This 4-4-0 locomotive, No. 104, was built at the Hazelton Shops in 1876.

LEADVILLE, COLORADO   Colorado Midland

Here is the Colorado Midland's station at Leadville in the 1900s. The road's herald can be seen on the lower part of the chimney and Pikes Peak Route is on the triangle above.   *Library, State Historical Society of Colorado.*

Engine No. 53 might have stopped at this mining town.

LEBANON, KENTUCKY (1857)   Louisville & Nashville

Here is the "South Atlantic Limited" about to leave Lebanon on the Louisville-Corbin run behind Class K-1 Pacific No. 174 about 1915. The historic brick station was built in 1857, and in the far portion of the building locomotives were housed overnight during runs between Lebanon and Louisville sixty-seven miles away. The old hotel opposite the station was torn down to make room for a new passenger station in the 1920s.   *L. & N.*

LEBANON, PENNSYLVANIA (1880s)   Cornwall & Lebanon

This was quite an imposing station for a short-line railroad in the 1880s. From Conewago, on the Pennsylvania's main line east of Harrisburg, the line was twenty-two miles long.

LOS GATOS, CALIFORNIA   Southern Pacific >

The South Pacific Coast was a narrow-gauge railroad nicknamed the "Picnic Line," acquired by the Southern Pacific in 1887 and made standard gauge in 1906. This picture at Los Gatos was taken before the changeover and shows plenty of "Picnickers."   *Railroad Magazine.*

LINCOLN, NEBRASKA (1880s)　　　　　　Chicago, Burlington & Quincy

Two freight stations and a passenger depot behind the "Eating House" constituted the Burlington's facilities at Lincoln when this early picture was taken in the 1870s.　　　　　　*Nebraska State Historical Society.*

MADISONVILLE, KENTUCKY (1870s)　　　　　　Louisville & Nashville

Etched in the glass over the windows in the operator's bay is this station's name —Madisonville. The first station built there, it was replaced by a larger brick building in the 1920s and it is located on the St. Louis–Evansville–Nashville line.　　　　　　*L. & N.*

MANITOU, COLORADO   Manitou & Pikes Peak

Traveling to the summit of Pikes Peak via rack railway has been a popular tourist attraction since the 1880s. A nine-mile trip from the base station at Manitou brought passengers to the summit.   *Library, State Historical Society of Colorado.*

MEADVILLE, PENNSYLVANIA (1865)   Erie

Meadville was an important stop on the broad-gauge Atlantic & Great Western a hundred years ago. A hundred-room hotel and "a dining room as long as a train" were part of the railroad's facilities here. It has been described as the most celebrated station of the two-sided type.   *W. A. Lucas.*

No. 5 was typical of the locomotives that stopped at Meadville.

MESA, ARIZONA (1895)   Southern Pacific

This station was completed in time for the opening of the road into Mesa on December 1, 1895, and the picture was taken about that time.   *S. P.*

MILLBROOK, NEW YORK (1880)   New Haven

This was a station on the old Central New England Railroad, seventeen miles north of Hopewell. The photograph was taken about 1930, and the building was abandoned in 1938.   *Thomas Annin.*

MIDLAKE, UTAH   Southern Pacific

In 1902, to avoid a forty-four-mile-longer original route around the north end of Great Salt Lake, a causeway was built by the Southern Pacific across the lake. Some twenty miles of fill and twelve miles of trestle made up the new route, with Camp 20 becoming known as Midlake. A row of houses on pilings constituted a town which once had a population of thirty. Since 1945, with the trestle portion replaced by fill, Midlake on the Lucin Cut-Off has become another ghost town.
Railroad Magazine.

MINNEWAUKAN, NORTH DAKOTA (1885)　　　　　Northern Pacific

This was the first train into Minnewaukan on August 10, 1885, on the branch line from Jamestown to Leeds. The station sign reads "Northern Pacific Express Co."　　　　　*N. P.*

MONTEAGLE, TENNESSEE　　　　　Louisville & Nashville

In this 1900s scene, hacks have brought passengers from nearby mountain resort hotels to catch the local train to Cowan, fourteen miles away on the main line of the Nashville, Chattanooga & St. Louis. Monteagle is on the Tracy City Branch. The water tank with its ornate valance is as worthy of note as the station.　　*L. & N.*

MONTE VISTA, COLORADO

Denver & Rio Grande

On the Creede Branch of the Denver & Rio Grande, this was Monte Vista in the 1900s. *Library, State Historical Association of Colorado.*

MONTPELIER, VIRGINIA (1915)   Southern

Ninety miles south of Washington is Montpelier station, still kept in excellent repair. This town is where President Madison's house is located.

Southern locomotive No. 1214 is a 4-6-2 engine.   *So.*

MONTROSE, COLORADO   Denver & Rio Grande

As at Durango station, the three-foot and standard-gauge track is evident. Montrose is almost halfway between Denver and Ogden.

Library, State Historical Association of Colorado.

Note the size difference between the narrow-gauge locomotive No. 107 and the standard-gauge No. 772 which were photographed in Montrose in 1927.

MOORHEAD, MINNESOTA (1871)   Northern Pacific

This is the combination depot at Moorhead as it looked in the fall of 1876. This is one mile east of Fargo across the state line. The 4-4-0 locomotive without a pilot is in freight service.   *N. P.*

NORWICH, NEW YORK (1880s)   New York, Ontario & Western

On the N.Y.O. & W. main line, this was Norwich station in the 1900s.
                    Thomas Annin.

NEW WESTMINSTER, BRITISH COLUMBIA, CANADA　　　　　Great Northern

The International Limited makes a stop at New Westminster, fourteen miles east of Vancouver, in this photograph of the 1920s.

NORTH CONWAY, NEW HAMPSHIRE
Boston & Maine

The 1896 Excursion Book of the Pennsylvania Railroad says: "North Conway is situated at the southern entrance to the White Mountain region, 137 miles north of Boston." To collectors of toy or model trains, this station might almost appear as the prototype of one of the miniature models.

∨

OAKLAND, MARYLAND (1884) Baltimore & Ohio

This substantial brick station at Oakland is architecturally interesting because of its circular tower. There can be no mistaking its date for it appears just under the peak of the roof. *Brother Andrew.*

No. 1630, a 2-8-0 engine, is typical of the B. & O.'s motive power of the period.

OCEANSIDE, CALIFORNIA (1885)   Atchison, Topeka & Santa Fe

This station at Oceanside, ninety-seven miles south of Los Angeles, was built in 1885, and the picture here was taken in 1940. It was replaced by a new building in 1946.   *Santa Fe.*

Locomotive No. 1812, a 2-6-2 BLW engine, was built in 1906.

OKLAHOMA CITY, OKLAHOMA   Atchison, Topeka & Santa Fe

Although identified as above, if other data is correct, this was the freight station at Guthrie, some miles north, in 1904.   *Santa Fe.*

Locomotive No. 2 was completed in 1881 and cost $8,000.

ONEONTA, NEW YORK (1874)   Delaware & Hudson
   "Extensive shops are located here giving employment to about 1,000 men,"
says an old D. & H. brochure of Oneonta, the largest town between Binghamton
and Albany on the Susquehanna Division. This original station was replaced in
1892.

PEACE DALE, RHODE ISLAND (1870s)   Narragansett Pier Railroad

The Narragansett Pier line was an early summer resort line operating eight miles from Kingston where connection was made with the New York, New Haven & Hartford. Peace Dale was an intermediate station about midway.

Collection of Gerald M. Best.

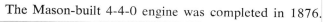

The Mason-built 4-4-0 engine was completed in 1876.

PINE CITY, MINNESOTA   Northern Pacific

Here is a train of the St. Paul & Duluth Railroad at Pine City, seventy-four miles east of Minneapolis en route to Duluth in 1883. This road later became a part of the Northern Pacific.   *N. P.*

PEEWEE VALLEY, KENTUCKY (1867)   Louisville & Nashville

This picture was taken on opening day of the new Peewee Valley station in 1867. About sixty people came to welcome No. 5 pulling a passenger train of the Louisville & Frankfort Railroad, which later became a part of the L. & N. in 1881. For the next forty years the station served as a community center, and "train time" was a happy time. Dozens of horse-drawn rigs came to meet commuters returning from a hard day at Louisville seventeen miles away, among them Milton H. Smith, President of the L. & N.   *L. & N.*

POCATELLO, IDAHO   Union Pacific

Most of the people appearing in this picture of Pocatello about 1885 appear to be railroad employees. Pocatello is 714 miles east of Portland and has always been an important stop on the U. P.'s main line.   *U. P.*

"Jupiter," Locomotive No. 82, was one of the engines which met at Promentory Point, Utah, for the driving of the golden spike which joined the Union Pacific and Central Pacific, the first transcontinental railroad, on May 10, 1869.

POINT OF ROCKS, MARYLAND (1875)   Baltimore & Ohio

Eighty miles west of Baltimore is Point of Rocks which the B. & O.'s "Main Stem" reached April 1, 1832. Further progress was delayed here for a while due to canal opposition. This was the second station at this location.   *Ray Brubacker.*

Locomotive No. 117 was known as the "Thatcher Perkins."

PROVO, UTAH (1877)   Union Pacific

This picture was made about ten years after the station at Provo was built. It is 47.5 miles south of Salt Lake City.   *U. P.*

RICHMOND, MASSACHUSETTS (1907)
Boston & Albany

The old Richmond station built in the late 1870s still stands behind the new building almost completed in 1907. Frederick A. Clement, the station agent, stands in the foreground.   *Thomas Annin.*

A 4-6-0 locomotive, No. 406, hauls a typical passenger train of the time.

RAWLINS, WYOMING (1868)   Union Pacific

Rawlins station was a few years old when this photograph was taken—a typical scene approaching train time.   *U. P.*

Representative of the kind of locomotive that stopped at Rawlins is No. 846, a 4-4-0 type engine.

RINGGOLD, GEORGIA (1850)　　　　Western & Atlantic

Since May 9, 1850, when the first train ran between Chattanooga and Atlanta, this depot at Ringgold has been in continuous use. The line was originally the Western & Atlantic Railroad, and the station was built in 1849 of local sandstone, the walls being fourteen inches thick. At that time Ringgold was a bigger market than Atlanta, and large quantities of wheat were shipped from there. On November 27, 1863, during the Civil War Battle of Ringgold, the building was struck by a shell, damaging the left corner. As shown in the picture, this was repaired with limestone blocks.

The station has changed little since April 12, 1862, when James J. Andrews and nineteen Yankee raiders rolled by with the locomotive "General" which they had stolen at Big Shanty eighty miles down the line. The "General" ran out of steam about two miles north of here and the raiders took to the hills.　　　　　　　　　　　　　　*L. & N.*

The 1914 painting by Wibur G. Kurtz pictures the locomotive "Texas" running in reverse in pursuit of the "General."

ROCKFORD, ILLINOIS
Rockford station on a cold winter morning about 1945. On the I. C. line to
Omaha, it was replaced by a new structure in 1954.

Illinois Central
Railroad Magazine.

ROCK SPRINGS, WYOMING   Union Pacific

Back in the 1870s, Rock Springs station on the U. P. main line between Omaha and Ogden presented this scene. One might wonder how long or how often the six chairs on the platform were occupied.   *U. P.*

ROCKWOOD, TENNESSEE (1890s)   Southern

On the former Queen & Crescent main line to Cincinnati, seventy miles north of Chattanooga, a photographer perpetuated this scene at Rockwood in the 1900s, evidently on a hot summer day. Unfortunately, as with so many old photographs, no story is known.   *So.*

SALEM, NEW YORK (1852)   Delaware & Hudson

The first station at Salem is pictured as it was about 1870. In this instance the roundhouse with its conical roof is more interesting than the station.

SALEM, OREGON   Southern Pacific
    Carriages and wagons are waiting for a train's arrival at Salem in this scene
about 1900.   *S. P.*

SHAMOKIN, PENNSYLVANIA (1876)   Philadelphia & Reading

This interesting 1876 drawing by architect Frank Furness was made for the proposed new station at Shamokin, Pennsylvania. On the Reading's division of the same name, Shamokin is 138 miles from Reading Terminal, Philadelphia, and 50 miles from Williamsport.

SHASTA SPRINGS, CALIFORNIA   Southern Pacific

An excursion group has just arrived at the northern California resort, Shasta Springs. The photograph was taken about 1910.

SILVERNAILS, NEW YORK (1880s)   New Haven

Some twenty miles northeast of Rhinecliff on the Hudson was this little station of the old Central New England Railroad, later incorporated into the New Haven. M. J. Wheeler, the agent shown in the picture, started here in 1893 and stayed until the line was abandoned in 1938.

SOMERSET, KENTUCKY   Southern

This is the agent's office in the country freight station at Somerset in 1903.
Frank Hanzsche and W. C. Shepard shown here were the staff.   *So.*

SOUTH SUPERIOR, WISCONSIN (1885)   Northern Pacific

This combination station was originally built at Ashland in 1885, but was moved to South Superior in 1892.

STURGIS, MICHIGAN   New York Central

Locomotive No. 149 stopped at Sturgis on the Lake Shore & Michigan Southern long enough for everyone to pose for the photographer, who took this picture in the 1870s.

TIMBER, OREGON (C. 1915)   Southern Pacific

The sign on the station at Timber reads: "To Tillamook 67 7/10 M., Elev. 978 feet, To San Francisco 793 1/10 M." This log-constructed building burned in 1960.

VICTOR, COLORADO   Midland Terminal

This picture of a station on fire is most unusual. It was on the old Midland Terminal Railroad, and the date was August 21, 1899.

Library, State Historical Society of Colorado.

WHITEHALL, NEW YORK   Delaware & Hudson

Whitehall station, seventy-eight miles north of Albany, is pictured about 1910. The depot is a division point for the Saratoga and Champlain Divisions. The State Barge Canal has its terminus at Whitehall.

The 4-4-0 camelback locomotive No. 443 pulls a milk train which might have stopped at Whitehall.

PART II

The Suburban Stations

*H*OW FAR SUBURBAN TERRITORY EXTENDS OUT FROM A CITY IS QUESTIONABLE. Perhaps traveling time of, say, up to one hour might be a better way of defining suburbia. On some lines one might travel almost sixty miles in this time, while on other roads only thirty or forty miles is possible. The greater proportion of such suburban travel would seem to be within this hourly limit although some commuters do travel further and longer.

Commuting by rail goes back over a hundred years, and special rates and tickets were in use even that long ago. The station, basically rural, gradually became geared to the morning and evening rushes for which, of course, railroad management had to plan. Half a century ago streetcar lines brought city-bound people to the stations in the larger communities where now parking spaces have to be provided. Many old buildings have been removed and replaced by others, little more than shelters.

Despite occasional or even frequent inconveniences (depending on the locality), travel by this form of mass transport is certainly less trying on the nerves than bucking highway traffic at the rush hour. It's usually less expensive, too. One wonders why or how those who could use the train, if convenient to their occupation, do drive under today's circumstances.

But, back to yesterday's commuters—here are some of their stations when life was less hurried.

ARDSLEY-ON-HUDSON, NEW YORK   New York Central

These pictures taken in the early 1900s show Ardsley-on-Hudson, twenty-two miles from Grand Central. Not only was this a suburban station but also a country hotel, seen in the background and connected to the station by a footbridge. The complex was an asset of the community. There was even a dock on the Hudson River. The sign over the porte cochere reads, "Notice to automobilers—automobiles are positively forbidden to pass through the entrance to this station except for the purpose of taking on or discharging passengers."   *N. Y. C.*

Locomotive No. 3368 is a 4-6-2 engine, seen a few miles north of Ardsley. ➤

116

BEDFORD PARK, NEW YORK   New York Central

Better known since the early 1900s as Bedford, this station on the Harlem Division is about forty miles from Grand Central, between Mt. Kisco and Katonah. This old station of the 1870s has since been replaced. Even the old flatcars were lettered New York and Harlem when this photograph was taken.   *N.Y.C.*

BRYN MAWR, PENNSYLVANIA   Pennsylvania Railroad ❯

One of Philadelphia's best-known suburban towns is Bryn Mawr, ten miles from Broad Street Station. This stone building of the 1870s was famous and often pictured, and only recently succumbed to "progress," when it was replaced by a small utilitarian structure. The pictures indicate that, long ago, the P.R.R. proudly publicized it.

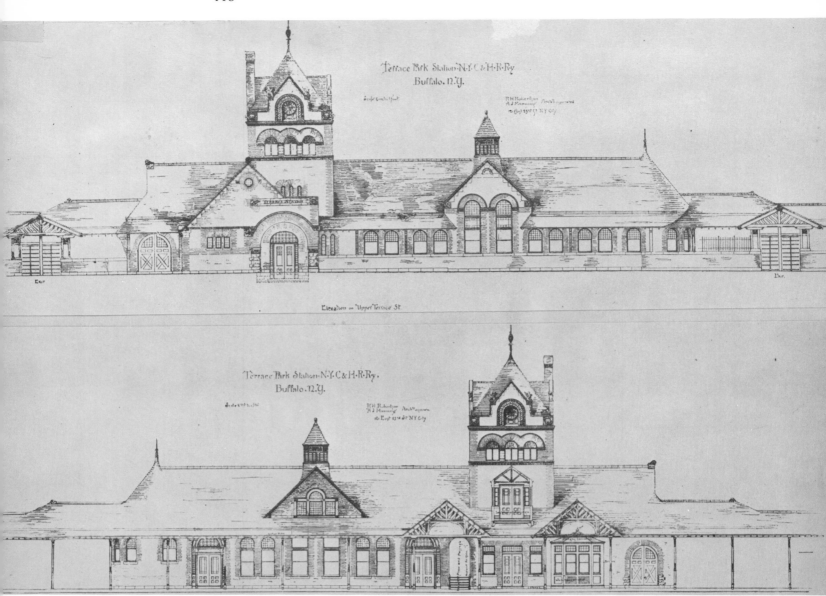

Terrace Park Station N.Y.C & H.R.R.Ry.
Buffalo, N.Y.

Elevation on Upper Terrace St.

Terrace Park Station N.Y.C & H.R.R.Ry.
Buffalo, N.Y.

NEW YORK CENTRAL LINES

9208

CROTON LAKE, NEW YORK   New York Central

This is one of the smallest flag stations on the Putnam Division, thirty-three miles from Grand Central but within commuting range. The photograph was taken in the 1920s.

<

BUFFALO, TERRACE PARK STATION, NEW YORK (1887)   New York Central

Terrace Park station in Buffalo was designed by architects R. H. Robertson and A. D. Manning and built in 1887. It was described as "a very large and handsome structure, with stone base, pressed brick walls, terra cotta trimmings and a tile roof." These contemporary architect's drawings bear this out.

No. 9208—a class F-103-A engine—was manufactured in Pittsburgh in 1909.

ELWOOD, MISSOURI   Missouri Pacific

   Here is one of St. Louis's suburban stations five miles from Union Station as it
looked about 1900.   *Mo. Pac.*

ENGLEWOOD, NEW JERSEY   Erie

Fourteen miles north of Jersey City is Englewood. Originally on the Northern Railroad of New Jersey, this station was photographed in the 1870s. The railroad was a six-foot or wide-gauge line as was its successor, the Erie.   *Thomas Annin.*

ENGLEWOOD, NEW JERSEY   Erie

This is Englewood station, another building of course, as it appeared about 1900. The wide-gauge track had been changed to standard many years before.

GLEN RIDGE, NEW JERSEY (1887)   Delaware, Lackawanna & Western

An 1892 description of the Glen Ridge stations says, "The railroad passes through a sandstone cut eighteen feet deep so that a wagon-road is on a level with the upper story of the building. In addition to its use for a railroad depot, the building had to be designed to accommodate a Post Office and an express office. . . . The wide porch roof at the front . . . is extended at one end so as to form a porte cochere."

Architect Jesse H. Lockwood's drawing shows the hillside location and lower level as well as the plans.

This photograph was made at the upper level about 1900: the left-hand sign has "Post Office" and that at the right "Glen Ridge." *Thomas Taber.*

Locomotive No. 1116 is a 4-6-2 engine and was photographed in 1926.

HAWTHORNE, NEW YORK   New York Central

On the Central's Harlem Division, this was Hawthorne in the 1900s, twenty-eight miles from New York. The CH on the sign is Chatham, ninety-nine miles north.
N. Y. C.

LAKE HOPATCONG, NEW JERSEY   Delaware, Lackawanna & Western

Within the suburban New York area, and also a resort community, Lake Hopatcong is forty-two miles from New York. This station, built about 1912, is a good example of the excellent stone structures built by the Lackawanna in most of its commuting territory. About the time of completion, when this picture was taken, there was a boat landing on the canal shown and one could go by this means to various lake landings. This station should also be included in Part V because it is now a realtor's office.   *Thomas Taber.*

A 4-6-0 engine No. 1070 pulls a commuter train.

JENKINTOWN, PENNSYLVANIA   Reading

One of the busiest suburban stations in the Philadelphia area is this one at Jenkintown, only eleven miles from Reading Terminal. The line to the right in the picture is the main line to New York while to the left is the Bethlehem Branch. This is how the station appeared in the 1900s. Another stone building has replaced it, and the lines were electrified in the 1930s.

LANGHORNE, PENNSYLVANIA   Reading

On the Reading's New York Division twenty-four miles from Reading Terminal, this was Langhorne about 1890. This has always been a busy commuting station. In 1909, for instance, over fifty trains a day stopped here, and today there are still almost as many. The old inn in the background is still in business.

LANSDALE, PENNSYLVANIA   Reading

This view of Lansdale, twenty-four miles from Philadelphia, was taken about 1890. A note about the planting is in order. Like a few other railroads, the Reading maintained flower beds and shrubbery at most of its stations and had its own greenhouse and nursery for many years.

Representative of the type of locomotive that stopped at Lansdale is No. 453, a 4-4-0 engine, which was photographed in 1886.

LONG BRANCH, NEW JERSEY   Central Railroad of New Jersey

This is the west end of the Long Branch station about 1900. Originally a summer resort forty miles from Jersey City, it has become more of a suburban town since this picture was taken. The horse-drawn hotel omnibuses are very much in evidence, a common form of transportation then.   *Thomas Annin.*

LOWELL, MASSACHUSETTS   Boston & Maine

Within the commuting area of Boston, twenty-five miles away, this is Lowell station in 1906. The New Haven also used this station in bygone days.

MORRISTOWN, NEW JERSEY   Delaware, Lackawanna & Western

There have been five stations built by the Lackawanna at Morristown, the first about 1838 to 1846, the second in the late 1840s, and this is the third as it looked in the 1870s.   *Thomas Annin.*

Morristown station as it appeared in the early 1900s is shown here. The community was known as the wealthiest on the Lackawanna, and the railroad, beginning in 1883, ran a train for particular commuters, which became famous as the "Millionaire's Express." To mark its twentieth anniversary in 1903, its patrons took the entire train crew to a testimonial dinner while their wives did likewise with the crew's wives. The Lackawanna has always had a close, friendly relationship between passengers and crews, and this still exists today. The present station was built about 1916.

NEW YORK CITY, HIGH BRIDGE   New York Central

Where the Putnam Division turns north from the Central's main line along the Harlem River is High Bridge. Named for the bridge seen in the background, it is seven miles from Grand Central.

According to *Locomotive Engineering* in 1899, the train passing under High Bridge is the Saratoga Limited on its first trip June 24, 1899. The cars were Wagner Palace cars hauled by locomotive 907, and the photograph was taken by F. W. Blauvelt.

NEW YORK CITY, 138TH STREET   New York Central

Designed by Robertson & Manning, the 138th Street station in the Bronx on the Central's Harlem Division was an unusually picturesque building. Combining a clock tower, entrance and other arches, conical platform roof ends, a footbridge, and other features it was undeniably different. It was the first station in the Bronx after crossing the Harlem River and was five miles from Grand Central.   *N. Y. C.*

PEEKSKILL, NEW YORK   New York Central

Forty miles north of the terminal, the next station beyond the end of electrification at Harmon is Peekskill. This is the station about 1910.

The Peekskill local is shown on its way to its destination.

PHILADELPHIA, CHELTEN AVENUE, PENNSYLVANIA   Pennsylvania Railroad

This is Chelten Avenue station eight miles from Broad Street station on the Chestnut Hill Branch about 1905. This line has always been a busy one serving the northwest section of the city.

PHILADELPHIA, CHESTNUT HILL, PENNSYLVANIA   Reading

The Reading's Chestnut Hill Branch terminal was built in the 1880s. It was a complete terminal in the days of steam, having a five-stall roundhouse, water tank, coaling dock, and other facilities. These photographs were taken in the 1930s shortly before the station was replaced by a new one, and the line electrified.

No. 383 was typical of the locomotives that came to Chestnut Hill.

PHILADELPHIA, UPSAL, PENNSYLVANIA   Pennsylvania Railroad

Nine miles from the terminal on the Chestnut Hill Branch is Upsal. This photograph was taken in the 1890s and shows the type of locomotive used then in suburban service, a 4-4-0 of the old P class.

PHILADELPHIA, WALNUT LANE, PENNSYLVANIA   Reading

This was the Walnut Lane Station on the Reading's Chestnut Hill Branch in the 1880s, almost eight miles from Reading Terminal. The name of this station was later changed to Washington Lane and a new brick station was built. It is today one of the busy commuter stations on the branch.

PHILADELPHIA, WISSAHICKON, PENNSYLVANIA   Reading

Only six and a half miles from Reading Terminal, this station on the Norristown Branch was pictured in the 1880s. The photograph was evidently taken when the station was new, as the grading does not appear to have been finished for the porte cochere at the far side.

>

ST. LOUIS, TUCKER'S STATION, MISSOURI   Missouri Pacific

On the old Iron Mountain Railroad, now part of the Missouri Pacific, this station called Tucker's is nominated as the most unusual of all suburban stations. Located at the foot of what is now Iaska Street, and also known as Carondelet, it was built for commuters and literally clings to the high cliff along the Mississippi.

Locomotive No. 1605 of the 4-6-0 type was built by Brooks Dunkirk Works in 1901.

SALEM, MASSACHUSETTS (1847)   Boston & Maine

One of the most picturesque of all stations was this one at Salem built in 1847 by Gridley J. F. Bryant. This view was made more than fifty years later. Carroll Meeks describes it thus: "The flattened arch over the tracks is flanked by a pair of towers which can be interpreted as either villa or Norman style. The polygonal masonry adds another curious note of historicism with its air of seeking the primitive." This, too, unfortunately fell before the march of "progress."

Dr. David K. Lovely.

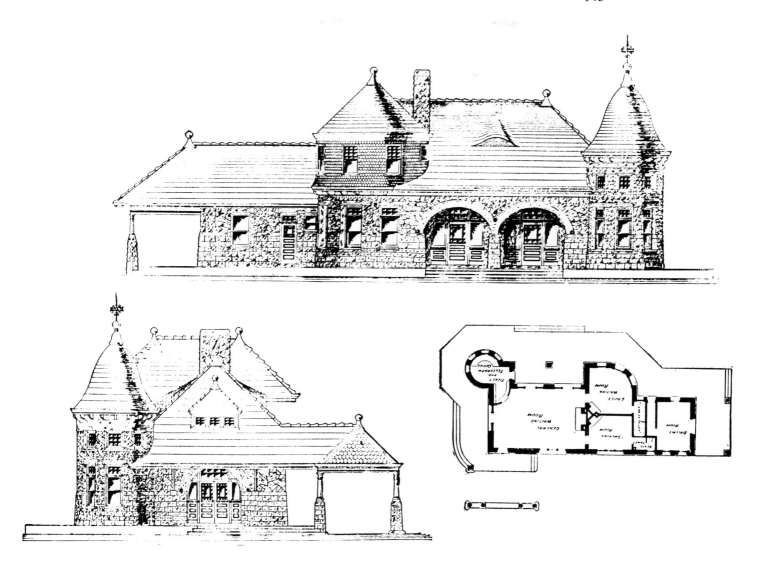

SOMERVILLE, NEW JERSEY   Central Railroad of New Jersey

Built in the 1880s to the design of architect Frank V. Bodine, this Somerville station is thirty-four miles from Jersey City. The construction is stone with a slate roof, and there were railroad offices on the second floor. The drawing is the architect's work.

No. 789, a 4-6-0 camelback, pulls an eleven-car commuter train.

TRENTON JUNCTION, NEW JERSEY (1876)   Reading

The Delaware & Bound Brook in New Jersey and the Northern Pennsylvania Railroad in Pennsylvania built and opened a line in time to bring excursionists from New York to the Philadelphia Centennial Exhibition in 1876. This was their station at Trenton Junction, opened that year. These roads were acquired by the Philadelphia & Reading in 1879, and the photograph dates to the 1880s. The "clock tower" is an unusual and interesting feature of this building.

A branch line to the center of Trenton diverged here. When a new station was built about the 1920s the name was changed to West Trenton. The Reading's electrified territory on the New York Division ends here, thirty-three miles from Reading Terminal.

Reading

YORKTOWN HEIGHTS, NEW YORK   New York Central
   Some forty-two miles from Grand Central is this little station on the Putnam
Division.

PART III

The Smaller and Medium-Size City Stations

THERE IS, OF COURSE, NO ARBITRARY DIVISION BY POPULATION OR OTHERWISE FOR this grouping of stations. It does serve, however, to illustrate a size or type of medium-sized buildings in communities which had grown from rural dimensions. Today, many are in the larger city class, and some are even state capitals.

In the railroad expansion years when so many structures were being built, hotels were often part of the station building or immediately adjoined it. Perhaps the Baltimore & Ohio did more than most in this field, President Garrett favoring such building combinations as at Cumberland and Grafton. Many became famous for their food or accommodations, and those at resorts or watering places were especially favored. At most stations in this category, at least a restaurant or lunchroom was provided if not rooms for travelers. On western lines, the name Harvey House was the magic word for food.

Sometimes these buildings housed railroad offices and other facilities, such as at division points or railroad towns where shops were located.

It seems unlikely that more, if any, of this type or size of building are in prospect except possibly where mass transportation might be sufficient to warrant it. These examples then, belong almost exclusively to the past.

ALBUQUERQUE, NEW MEXICO　　　　　　　　Atchison, Topeka & Santa Fe

The mission or Spanish style of architecture was adapted for this station of the Santa Fe at Albuquerque, pictured about 1910.

ALLIANCE, OHIO (1853)　　　　　　　　Pennsylvania Railroad

The original station at Alliance was designed by Solomon M. Roberts, Chief Engineer of the Fort Wayne & Chicago Railroad, and was built in 1853. Its architecture with gables and tower was interesting enough to warrant this early lithograph.

On December 8, 1856, a train for Chicago had just started when it was "broad-sided" by one on the Cleveland & Pittsburgh line arriving from Wellsville, demolishing a car in its center and killing eleven persons and injuring twenty-one. The photograph was taken shortly afterwards with the Chicago train still in place.

The accident was important in that it caused Ohio to pass a stop-and-proceed regulation for trains approaching crossings. This station was destroyed by fire in 1863. Both railroads are now part of the Pennsylvania.

Locomotive No. 210 was rebuilt at Altoona in 1868.

150

ALTOONA, PENNSYLVANIA (1854)   Pennsylvania Railroad

On a site selected in 1849, the Pennsylvania Railroad planned what was to be the city of Altoona and the location of its principal shops. On February 5, 1854, it was incorporated as a borough, and train service to Pittsburgh via the new line and tunnel at Gallitzin was established. The station and adjoining Logan House Hotel were completed about this same date.

ALTOONA, PENNSYLVANIA   Pennsylvania Railroad

The Logan House, "one of the finest hotels in the U.S., was opened by the railroad company to accommodate the immense travel over its line." The ornate ironwork illustrated shows only a part of the decor. A corner of the roof of the three-story building appears above the portico.

ASHEVILLE, NORTH CAROLINA (1880s)   Southern

The station at Asheville, North Carolina's famous resort, is shown here as it looked about 1890.   *Arthur Hampton Collection.*

Engine No. 338 was built by the Baldwin Locomotive Works.

AUSTIN, TEXAS   Missouri Pacific

The train is taking on passengers, and the locomotive will be backing to it shortly in this scene at Austin in the late 1870s. The Missouri Pacific tore down this station and built another two-story one with a tower in 1888, following in 1948 with a third one-story brick structure.

One of the first "Pacific" type locomotives, No. 1118 was completed in 1902.

BERKELEY, CALIFORNIA   Southern Pacific

The picture date is 1903 although the station at Berkeley is years older. All but two of the signs on the buildings are realtors' advertising.

No. 1437 is typical of the type of locomotive that stopped at Berkeley.

BETHLEHEM, PENNSYLVANIA   Reading

The old Union Station at Bethlehem used by the Reading and the Lehigh Valley looked like this in the 1890s. A new building replaced this one in 1925 and it, in turn, ceased operation in 1961.

BINGHAMTON, NEW YORK   Delaware & Hudson

The Delaware & Hudson and the Erie Railroad used this station jointly. This picture is from the 1920s although the building dates from the 1880s.

No. 910 is a **D. & H.** 2-8-0 locomotive which may have passed through here.

The New Bridgeport Station, New York, New Haven & Hartford Railroad.

BRIDGEPORT, CONNECTICUT (1905)   New Haven

In 1905, the large Bridgeport station shown here was new. Designed by Warren
H. Briggs, the supervising architect, it was constructed of granite and brick with a
red slate roof. The contemporary drawings show its arrangement and plan.

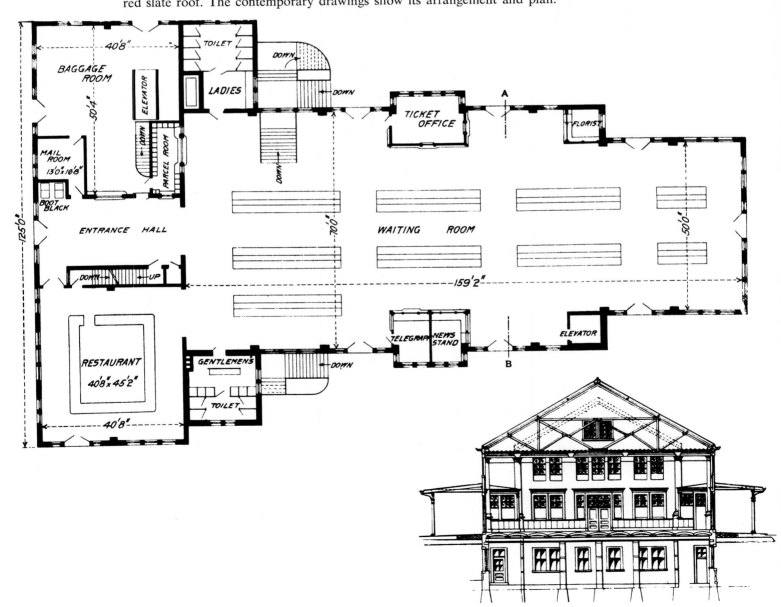

Seven years after the completion of the Bridgeport station, the New Haven electrified its main line from its connection with the Harlem Division of the New York Central below Mount Vernon to Stamford and to New Haven by 1914.

The 4-6-2 locomotive and the electric express show the range of trains that passed through the Bridgeport depot.

BURLINGTON, VERMONT   Rutland

In the early 1900s this Burlington station was a busy place, as this picture shows, with many conveyances and a four-wheeled trolley car awaiting debarking passengers. The cupolas for venting smoke are quite unusual and different from most train sheds. Lake Champlain is just visible to the left.

Engine 201 is representative of the kind of locomotive that stopped at Burlington.

CHATTANOOGA, TENNESSEE (1859)   Western & Atlantic

This is a photograph of the Chattanooga train shed by the Civil War photographer, George Barnard. Early railroads, now part of the Louisville & Nashville, which used this station were the Western & Atlantic, the East Tennessee & Georgia, and the Memphis & Charleston. It was designed by Eugene LeHardy and is recorded as having cost $38,000. It was used as a hospital during the war and is very similar to the Atlanta station destroyed by Sherman except that here only two tracks went through while at the wider Atlanta shed there were four. About one-third of this shed still stands.

L. & N.

Wilbur G. Kurtz painted the detailed study of "The Texas" as it appeared at the time of the Civil War.

CHAMBERSBURG, PENNSYLVANIA (1870s)   Cumberland Valley ❯

This is Chambersburg station in the 1870s. Its sign reads: "Martinsburg 42 miles, Harrisburg 52 miles." The Cumberland Valley, chartered in 1831, was one of the oldest railroads, the line between Chambersburg and Harrisburg being completed by 1837. It eventually became part of the Pennsylvania Railroad.

Passenger locomotive No. 30 is shown with its engineer and crew about 1894.

COLUMBUS, OHIO (1862)   Pennsylvania Railroad

Columbus is on the former Pittsburgh, Cincinnati, Chicago & Pittsburgh Railway, and this was the first Union Station built there in 1862. It was a frame structure with three through tracks, and stood until 1874. The car shops and, a bit nearer the camera, an early horse car are in this scene of about 1870.

A 4-4-0 locomotive, engine No. 90 was built in 1868.

COLUMBUS, OHIO (1875)   Pennsylvania Railroad

The second Union Station, a much larger brick building with apparently six through tracks, is pictured in the 1880s.

CUMBERLAND, MARYLAND   Baltimore & Ohio

This was the first station and hotel at Cumberland which the B. & O. reached on November 5, 1842, although the photograph dates from about the late 1850s. The wooden "splice bars" on the outside of the rails help date the photograph. A much larger hotel and station replaced this one in 1872.

DUBUQUE, IOWA   Illinois Central

The Illinois Central built this large brick station at Dubuque in 1887, and the photograph was taken shortly thereafter. The station was 290 feet long and 50 feet wide with offices upstairs. A major reconstruction was done in 1944.   *I. C.*

A long freight train travels an Illinois Central route.

DURAND, MICHIGAN   Canadian National, Ann Arbor Line ❯

Five locomotives are easily seen in this 1900s photograph taken at Durand where the Ann Arbor and Grand Trunk lines crossed. Actually a sixth engine is at the water tank. All those posed in this interesting scene are 4-4-0s.

EASTON, PENNSYLVANIA (1891)   Lehigh Valley

The Lehigh Valley's Easton station, built in 1891, was still unchanged when this picture was taken in 1920.

ELMIRA, NEW YORK (1875)   Erie
                                                Pennsylvania

Used by both the Pennsylvania and Erie Railroads, this Union Station, built in 1875, appeared like this in 1900.

ERIE, PENNSYLVANIA   Pennsylvania Railroad

This is the Philadelphia & Erie station at Erie built in the early 1860s. In 1877, a few years after this picture was taken, it was destroyed in a fire.

GALESBURG, ILLINOIS   Santa Fe

An architect's rendering shows the Galesburg station as it appeared in 1891.

GALESBURG, ILLINOIS   Chicago, Burlington & Quincy

A 1905 scene shows a Class K-3 locomotive No. 677 that has just arrived at Galesburg bringing an express train from Savanna on the Mississippi River. This depot burned in 1911.   *C. B. Q.*

Train No. 17, a fast mail of the Santa Fe, stops at Galesburg in 1900.

GRAND RAPIDS, MICHIGAN

Pennsylvania
New York Central
Chesapeake & Ohio

In the 1870s, the Grand Rapids & Indiana (now part of the Pennsylvania), the Michigan Southern (now New York Central) and the Pere Marquette (now Chesapeake & Ohio) used this station. The wide-spread, seven-windowed passenger car is unusual, as is the architecture of the building.

C. & O.

GREENFIELD, MASSACHUSETTS   Boston & Maine

On the B. & M.'s main line, 106 miles from Boston and 85 miles from Troy, the scene at Greenfield about 1900 is typical of train time.   *Thomas Annin.*

HARRISBURG, PENNSYLVANIA   Pennsylvania Railroad

Always a busy place, the station and train shed at Harrisburg appeared like this in 1896.

JACKSONVILLE, FLORIDA   Atlantic Coast Line

This is the terminal station of the Atlantic Coast Line (now Seaboard Coast Line) in 1926. It would seem that even over forty years ago parking was a problem in Florida's second largest city.

Engine No. 89 is typical of those that traveled the line to its terminal.

Seaboard Coast Line Railroad Company.

KNOXVILLE, TENNESSEE   Southern >

This old 1882 photograph describes its location as the corner of Gay and Jackson streets. The depot is at the left and roundhouse at the right of the overpass. These were buildings of the East Tennessee, Virginia & Georgia Railway, a Southern Railway predecessor.   *So.*

KNOXVILLE, TENNESSEE (1905)   Louisville & Nashville

The last train to use this L. & N. station, built in 1905, ran in March 1968. The division operating and traffic offices were in the building which will probably give way to urban renewal.   *D. E. MacGregor.*

L. & N. train No. 33, pulled by engine No. 277, is shown in 1929.   *L. & N.*

LOCKPORT, NEW YORK   New York Central

Representative of the substantial stone and brick buildings of the New York Central about seventy years ago is this station at Lockport as pictured in 1905. It is on the Rochester–Niagara Falls line.

MANCHESTER, NEW HAMPSHIRE   Boston & Maine

On the B. & M.'s line to Concord, this station at Manchester was built in the 1880s. The picture is dated 1900.

MONCTON, NEW BRUNSWICK, CANADA (1871)   Canadian National

Eighty miles north of St. John is Moncton, and in 1891 this is how the station appeared with the Intercolonial Railway's shops in the background. The four-wheel freight cars might even suggest that the photograph is earlier. The Intercolonial is now part of the Canadian National Railway.   *C. N.*

"Lady Elgin," locomotive No. 1, was built in Portland, Maine. It was photographed in 1853.   *C. N.*

OGDEN, UTAH (1886)

Denver & Rio Grande
Oregon Short Line
Southern Pacific
Union Pacific

This is the Union Station at Ogden designed by Van Brunt and Howe and completed in 1886. The building combined a number of facilities including a hotel and railroad offices. The photograph was made about 1920.

Library, State Historical Society of Colorado.

OTTUMWA, IOWA (1887)   Chicago, Burlington & Quincy

Architects Burnham & Root designed this station at Ottumwa which was built in 1887. It was 197 feet by 36 feet and had an express room, baggage room, hallway, men's waiting room, ticket office, ladies' waiting room, toilet rooms, lunch counter, dining room, kitchen, bakery, and laundry. On the second floor were offices, supplies, and living rooms, all of which would seem to indicate a fully self-sufficient installation. In 1950, this building was replaced by a modern station.

C. B. & Q.

The Fast Mail, pulled by 4-4-2 locomotive No. 2709, leaves the Ottumwa station in 1905.

About 1910 the Des Moines River almost reaches the doors of the Ottumwa
station.   *C. B. & Q.*

PITTSFIELD, MASSACHUSETTS   Boston & Albany

    Union Station at Pittsfield served both the Boston & Albany, and the New Haven. This photograph from the 1890s also shows a Pittsfield Electric Street Railway car.

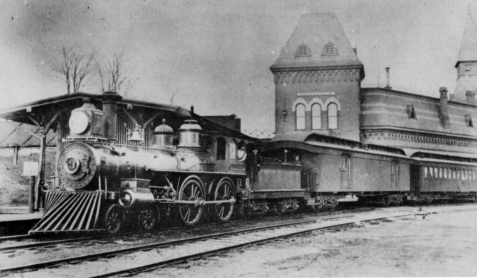

An 1890s photograph shows engine No. 3 and a passenger train at the Pittsfield depot. *Thomas Annin.*

1858

ROCHESTER, NEW YORK (1868)   New York Central

Although this picture is dated 1858, this view of Rochester station must be
at least ten years later because of the diamond-stacked engine and the clerestory-
roofed cars.

1882

New York Central Station, Rochester, N. Y.

ROCHESTER, NEW YORK (1882)   New York Central

 These pictures, taken in 1882 of the recently completed new station at Rochester, show the large train shed behind the building.

ROME, NEW YORK (1878)   New York Central

This is the Rome, Watertown & Ogdensburg station in 1878 where connection was made with the main line of the New York Central. The last car is probably the Wagner sleeping car for New York. The New York Central took over this road in 1891.

ST. JOHN, NEW BRUNSWICK, CANADA   Canadian National

Eighty miles south of Moncton is St. John, New Brunswick's largest city. Its Union Depot served the Intercolonial and Canadian Pacific when this picture was taken in the early 1900s.   *C. N.*

SAN ANTONIO, TEXAS   San Antonio & Aransas Pass

Pictured in the 1920s, this station at San Antonio was where Teddy Roosevelt entrained for his Cuban expedition with the Rough Riders in 1898. The San Antonio & Aransas Pass Railroad is now part of the Missouri Pacific.

Sixty years ago a night train, the "Davy Crockett" ran between here and Houston and advertised "wide vestibuled sleepers." It was known as the "Train That Is Always on Time."

No. 72, which ran on the San Antonio & Aransas Pass Railroad, was a 4-4-0 locomotive.

SANTA BARBARA, CALIFORNIA (1887)   Southern Pacific

This picture of the Southern Pacific's Santa Barbara station was taken about a dozen years after its opening in 1887. The old Pullman in this photograph was the "Matterhorn."

SCHENECTADY, NEW YORK   Delaware & Hudson

    This is a New York Central passenger train at Schenectady in 1871. The three tracks at the left are those of the Central and the one at the right the Delaware & Hudson's. The station is the building beyond Drullard's Hotel.   *D. & H.*

SIOUX CITY, IOWA   Elevated Railroad

Before even Chicago had an elevated railroad system, Sioux City, Iowa, with a population then of 20,000, had one, built in the late 1880s. About five miles long, two miles elevated and the rest at street level, it was double-tracked although only one engine and two coaches were the initial rolling equipment. The fare was five cents on the "El" and ten cents on the street level, and the cost of the project was $586,000. A few years later poles were put up for trolley wires, and Sioux City had another first—an electrified "El" system. Officially, the line was opened April 16, 1891, and it was operated for ten years, after which the surface lines were absorbed into the street railway system.   *Leonard Y. Tripp.*

SPRINGFIELD, MASSACHUSETTS (1870s)   Boston & Albany

The old brick train shed of the Springfield station had five tracks running through it in the 1870s. An 1891 picture shows only the center tracks remaining and both side arches closed in with doors and windows. The complete wording on the warning sign was, "Look Out For the Engine While the Bell Rings." Across the street was the four-story office building of the Boston & Albany, successor to the Western Railroad of Massachusetts and the Boston & Worcester.

The "Enfield," was built by Hinkley of Boston about 1872. The locomotive ran on the Springfield, Athol & North Eastern, which was bought by the Boston and Albany about 1880.

194

SYRACUSE, NEW YORK   New York Central

Part of the train shed shows in this view of the old Syracuse station in the 1880s. The first wagon at the curb has "U. S. Mail" lettering, and the others are evidently hotel omnibuses.   *N. Y. C.*

TAUNTON, MASSACHUSETTS (1865)   New Haven

   Taunton station was built in 1865, the design being influenced by Henry Holley.
Its details were Victorian Gothic, and one track ran under part of the building
with a train shed adjoining. In this view of the 1950s, two dormer windows formerly
on the left side of the roof are missing, the tower has been shortened, and the train
shed removed.   *N. H.*

   New Haven locomotive No. 1340, a 4-6-2, pulls a three-car train.

TOPEKA, KANSAS   Atchison, Topeka & Santa Fe

Waiting for the train at Topeka in 1880 are a crowd of local citizens and at least fourteen horse-drawn vehicles. The "Dining Hall" at the left of the building was the first of the famous Harvey House chain of restaurants established in 1875.

Santa Fe.

TRENTON, NEW JERSEY   Pennsylvania Railroad

The Trenton station was almost new in the 1890s when this picture was taken. The brick building behind it housed the offices of the old United Railroads of New Jersey and stood until fairly recently.

TRENTON, NEW JERSEY   Reading

The Reading's station in Trenton was a two-track, terminal depot at the end of a three-and-a-half-mile branch from the main line at West Trenton. This is a typical train at the station in the 1890s.   *Painting by George Bradshaw*

VICKSBURG, MISSISSIPPI (1907)   Illinois Central

Designed by D. H. Burnham & Company, this passenger station on Levee Street in Vicksburg was built in 1907. The picture was taken about the time of completion as the unpaved street indicates. The building is now used exclusively for the Vicksburg Division general offices.   *I. C.*

UTICA, NEW YORK   New York Central

This is the train for Boonville standing at the Utica station in 1865. The line was then the Utica & Black River Railroad which merged into the Rome, Watertown & Ogdensburg in 1886, finally becoming a part of the New York Central in 1891.

WATERTOWN, NEW YORK (1880s)   New York Central
    This is the old station at Watertown pictured in the early 1900s. It was torn
down and replaced with a larger building in 1910.
    Locomotive No. 3804 was typical of the type that passed through Watertown.

WORCESTER, MASSACHUSETTS (1875-77)   Boston & Albany

Designed by Ware and Van Brunt and completed under the supervision of Mr. E. S. Philbrick, Chief Engineer, this station has been described by Walter Berg as "a large terminal station, one of the best known structures of the kind in this country owing to its original design and bold methods of construction, the entrance to the train shed being spanned by a segmental arch with an opening of nearly 120 feet in width." The slender tower was also noteworthy.

WINNIPEG, MANITOBA, CANADA   Canadian Pacific

The first scheduled Canadian Pacific train to cross the continent arrives at
Winnipeg July 1, 1886, in this scene. It left Montreal June 28 and arrived at Port
Moody, British Columbia, on July 4.   *C. P.*

Westbound train No. 115 leaves Winnipeg in 1934.

PART IV

Stations and Terminals of the Large Cities

THE RAILROADS HAVE SOME JUSTIFICATION FOR SPENDING SO MUCH MONEY on their passenger terminals. Not the least is the fact that the railway passenger station is the main entrance to and exit from the city. Civic pride demands a fitting gateway and it is in the best interests of the railroad to do its share. The average passenger station has rarely retained its adequacy more than twenty-five to thirty years. It has been practically impossible to anticipate the exact degree of growth of business, and the cases are few where the railroads with all their foresight have been able to anticipate the future sufficiently. That explains why many of the stations now being built seem so enormous. It is quite possible that twenty-five years from now we shall look upon them, as magnificent as they now seem, as relics of a bygone age, woefully inadequate and out of date."

The above is a 1916 commentary on big city stations from *Passenger Terminals and Trains* (see Bibliography), and contains more than a little prophecy. To which, however, another sentence from the same source should be added:

"Magnificent stations do not earn one cent more of revenue, their cost is great, and they are costly to maintain, but if these mighty edifices will please the public, they must be built."

The following illustrations will serve, then, as a tribute to the last of their race.

206

ALBANY, NEW YORK (1900)   New York Central
                                           Delaware & Hudson

Albany's new station was opened in December 1900, and a busy place it was
for many years. In its first year there were 96 trains daily (New York Central—42,
Boston & Albany—10, Delaware & Hudson—31, and West Shore—13). During
the war years of 1942 and 1943, passenger traffic reached its peak when 121 trains
were handled daily. To Albany came the politicians from all over the state—groups
for legislative hearings, and candidates for elections—and most came and went
through this station. Its bar and restaurant were famous as social and business
centers. December 1968, saw the end of service—now 30 trains a day use a
new, small station across the Hudson.

ALBANY, NEW YORK   Delaware & Hudson

Not literally a station but the office building of the Delaware & Hudson, this structure is so architecturally interesting that it is well worth inclusion here. The occasion was the display of a new locomotive, No. 652, a 4-6-2 type, in 1929.

Railroad Magazine.

ATLANTA, GEORGIA (1853)   Western & Atlantic

At the time of the Civil War two railroads, the Western & Atlantic and the Georgia Railroad, used the Atlanta Union station which was built in 1853. The scene here is in September 1864, where alongside the train shed are boxcars loaded with household goods about to leave, complying with Sherman's order evacuating Atlanta's inhabitants. His own words written September 17 were, "I take the ground that Atlanta is a conquered place, and I propose to use it purely for our own military purposes, which are inconsistent with its habitation by the families of a brave people. I am shipping them *all*, and by next Wednesday the town will be a real military town, with no women boring me every order I give."

Library of Congress.

In the upper right-hand corner of this photograph, showing the destroyed roundhouse with some serviceable engines after the war, is this small wooden passenger station that served Atlanta at that time.

This was the end of the railroad depot at Atlanta—the wreckage of the train shed destroyed by Sherman's order. His policy: "The railroad station as the heart of the modern artery of business was second only in importance to the buildings and institutions of the confederate government itself, as a subject for elimination."

L. & N.; Library of Congress.

ATLANTA, GEORGIA: UNION STATION (1905)   Southern
                                             Seaboard
                                             Atlanta & West Point

   This Union Station at Atlanta was built in 1905, although the photograph was taken about 1940. The tracks of three railroads came into this terminal—the Southern, the Atlanta & West Point, and the Seaboard. Its architect was P. Thornton Marye, and its builders were Gude and Walker. A large train shed was taken down in 1925, and its towers were shortened before World War II. Its cost was $1.6 million. The Inman Yards are in the background.   *So.*

This Southern 4-6-2 locomotive and passenger train was typical of those that served Atlanta.

BALTIMORE, MARYLAND: CAMDEN STATION (1853)   Baltimore & Ohio

In 1852 the Baltimore & Ohio planned a monumental station for Baltimore, purchasing three city squares between Eutaw and Howard streets for the site. J. R. Niernsee and J. R. Nielson were the architects, and they designed it in the Italian style although "Normanesque" was also used in its description. When completed in 1853, it was the largest station in America. Wings were added in 1869 and later the central tower was shortened to the appearance as pictured.

A horsecar, No. 260, awaits debarking passengers outside Camden Station in 1893.   *B. & O.*

BALTIMORE, MARYLAND: CALVERT STATION (1850)   Pennsylvania Railroad

Begun in 1848, Calvert Station was built by the Baltimore & Susquehanna Railroad and opened in 1850. The architects were Niernsee and Neilson, and part of their own description of the building was as follows: "When completed, the depot will consist of a car house 315 feet long, 112 feet wide, occupying the diagonal of the square of ground owned by the company, and terminated at the end on Calvert Street by a large building, with a front of 112 feet, in the Italian style, 2 stories in height, containing the principal passenger entrance, ticket office, transportation and other offices. . . ."

It is interesting to note that in April 1861, an armed force of the State of Maryland took possession of this station while others, led by officials of Baltimore, destroyed bridges and property of the Northern Central. Much damage was sustained by this road during the conflict. This road was acquired in 1874 by the Pennsylvania.

BALTIMORE, MARYLAND: UNION STATION (1886)   Pennsylvania Railroad

Baltimore's first Union Station was opened in 1873 and served the Philadelphia, Wilmington & Baltimore, the Northern Central and Baltimore & Potomac of the Pennsylvania System, and the Western Maryland. Additions were made in 1882 but increased business dictated larger facilities, and the second Union Station illustrated was completed in 1886. Twenty-five years later, the present Union Station was opened, replacing the 1886 structure.

BALTIMORE, MARYLAND (1911)   Pennsylvania Railroad

The Pennsylvania's passenger facilities in Baltimore were combined in 1911 into a Union Station serving, in addition to its main line, the Northern Central and Western Maryland. This picture was taken about the time of completion, as construction materials not yet removed would indicate.

BIRMINGHAM, ALABAMA (1871)   Louisville & Nashville

The City of Birmingham came into being in 1870, and in 1871 the Relay House Hotel shown here was built, serving also as the city's first railroad station.   *L. & N.*

This 1871 photograph shows a locomotive of the type that served the original Birmingham station.

BIRMINGHAM, ALABAMA (1887)   Louisville & Nashville

In 1887 this Union Station designed by H. Wolters was built at 20th Street and Morris Avenue. The station proper is on the far side of the train shed in this picture.   *L. & N.*

Engine No. 95, built in the Louisville & Nashville's shops and decorated for the occasion, pulled the first train into the new Birmingham station in 1887. Here is how it looked posing in front of the train shed.   *L. & N.*

Drawn by Thornton Oakley.

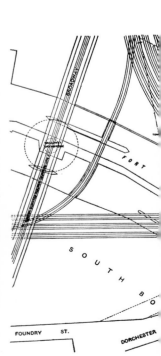

BOSTON, MASSACHUSETTS: SOUTH STATION (1898)   Boston & Albany
New Haven

    South Station was designed by Shepley, Rutan, and Coolidge and built in 1898 as a combined terminal for the New Haven and the Boston & Albany roads. It had twenty-eight tracks and a concourse, initially open but later enclosed, 620 feet long and 130 feet wide. It was for years the largest and busiest station in the country. For example, in the year ending June 30, 1916, it handled 38 million passengers, about 16 million more than Grand Central.

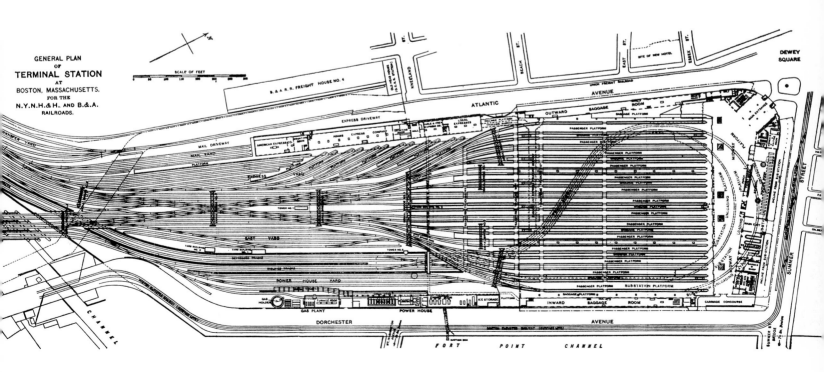

GENERAL PLAN OF TERMINAL STATION AT BOSTON, MASSACHUSETTS. FOR THE N.Y.N.H.&H. AND B.&A. RAILROADS.

BOSTON, MASSACHUSETTS: SOUTH STATION

Boston & Albany
New Haven

In 1931 a modernization program costing $2.5 million was undertaken, the old train shed removed and butterfly sheds installed, and many innovations added. Some 466 scheduled and many unscheduled trains were in operation at that time.

Courtesy New Haven Railroad.

BOSTON, MASSACHUSETTS: NORTH STATION (1893-94)   Boston & Maine

This picture from the 1900s shows the Boston & Maine's North Station. The earlier Boston & Lowell station can be seen on the left. A new station replacing both of these was built in 1928.   *Thomas Annin.*

CHICAGO, ILLINOIS (1848)   Chicago & North Western

Chicago's first station was built in 1848 by the Galena & Chicago Union Railroad, now part of the Chicago & North Western. It was located at Canal and Kinzie streets, half a mile from the present station at Canal and Madison streets. This is its appearance in 1849 after a second story had been added to provide office space.

C. & N. W.

The first locomotive in Chicago was this Galena & Chicago Union Railroad "Pioneer," built by Baldwin.

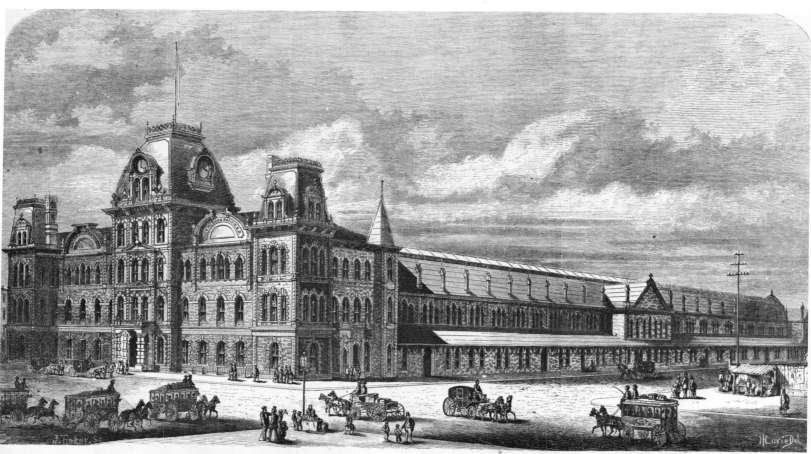

MICHIGAN SOUTHERN AND ROCK ISLAND PASSENGER DEPOT.

CHICAGO, ILLINOIS (1871)   Michigan Southern and Rock Island

The "Passenger Depot" of the Michigan Southern and Rock Island was completed just in time for the great Chicago fire and this old engraving shows it as built.

CHICAGO, ILLINOIS (1872)   Michigan Southern and Rock Island

After the great fire, the station was immediately rebuilt with some changes which can be noted by comparing the two pictures. The new opening was on October 25, 1872, and the train shed was converted to a temporary "coliseum" for forty-eight hours to present a series of Jubilee Concerts by Gilmore's Band in commemoration of the rehabilitation of the city. This is also known as La Salle Street Station.   *Rock Island Lines.*

Locomotive No. 926, a 4-6-2, pulls a Rock Island passenger train in 1926.

UNION PASSENGER STATION, CHICAGO, ILL.

CHICAGO, ILLINOIS: UNION STATION (1881)

Pittsburgh, Ft. Wayne & Chicago
Pittsburgh, Cincinnati, Chicago & St. Louis
Alton
Chicago, Milwaukee & St. Paul
Chicago, Burlington & Quincy

It was a busy scene around the new Union Station after it opened in 1881 according to this old lithograph. Its construction was a joint enterprise of five railroads. It was on the east side of Canal Street between Madison and Van Buren.

Engine No. 91 is typical of those that were seen at Chicago Union Station.

This photograph shows the south end of Union Station later in the 1880s.
Courtesy the Milwaukee Road.

CLEVELAND, OHIO (1854)

This old engraving illustrates the first station in Cleveland which opened in 1854. Six railroads used the station.   *N. Y. C.*

DENVER, COLORADO   Kansas Pacific >
                                                                                      Denver Pacific
                                                                                      Colorado Central

Denver's first station is shown in this old woodcut. In the 1870s the Kansas Pacific, Denver Pacific, and Colorado Central converged here.

Library, State Historical Society of Colorado.

DENVER, COLORADO: UNION STATION   6 Railroads

This is a view from 17th Street looking towards the Denver Union Station about 1905 with the Mizpah or welcome arch framing the entrance.

The track side was a scene of activity in another 1905 scene.

KANSAS CITY, MISSOURI: UNION STATION (1910)

Twelve railroads, all that enter Kansas City, own equally the Kansas City Terminal Company which operates this Union Station. Built at a cost of $11 million in 1910, it has sixteen through passenger tracks. The overall building dimensions are 510 feet by 150 feet with the extension over the tracks 410 feet by 165 feet. The photograph dates from the 1920s.

LOS ANGELES, CALIFORNIA: LA GRANDE (1893) Atchison, Topeka & Santa Fe
   The Santa Fe originally reached Los Angeles in 1885 via Colton through a
trackage arrangement with the Southern Pacific. A temporary station was built and
used from 1887 until the La Grande station was opened in 1893. At the junction
of Santa Fe Avenue and First Street, it was of Moorish design.   *S. F.*
No. 1342, a 4-6-2 type locomotive, arrives at Los Angeles in 1939.
                                                                R. W. Merriman.

Here are the track and platform side of La Grande station with a train just leaving in 1899.

LOUISVILLE, KENTUCKY (1891)　　　　　　　　　Louisville & Nashville

Louisville's Union Station was designed by architect F. W. Mowbray and opened in 1891. Its interior has been described as being one of the most elegant of its time. The domed, waiting-room ceiling arched four-and-a-half stories to a stained glass skylight, and each end of the room had a twenty-foot diameter rose window. The Louisville & Nashville, Pennsylvania, and Indianapolis & Louisville lines came into this station.

One of the first of many celebrities to use the station was Sarah Bernhardt, who arrived about a month after the grand opening. She consented to try her famous voice in the cavernous confines of the vast waiting room. Echoes ricochetting off the Tennessee marble trim played havoc with her dramatic rendition. Piqued, she flounced out in a huff, boarded a waiting carriage, and drove off to her hotel.

On July 15, 1905, the station burned as fifteen to twenty thousand people watched "a spectacle of almost unequaled grandeur in the history of Louisville fires." The two-foot-thick stone walls remained virtually intact, and the station was rebuilt within them.　　　　　　　　　　　　　　　　　　　　　　*L. & N.*

"The Jacksonian," a Chicago-Florida winter-season train stops at Louisville on its inaugural run in December 1941. It was operated jointly by L. & N., P. R. R., and A. C. L., but World War II traffic ended its running after the winter of 1942.

L. & N.

MEMPHIS, TENNESSEE   Southern

This is the Memphis station of the Memphis & Charleston Railroad, now part of the Southern, as it was in the 1880s.   *So.*

The yards near the Memphis & Charleston Railroad station of the 1880s show a variety of rolling stock. Half a dozen ancient engines are in front of the engine house, and one wishes that close-ups of each were available.   *So.*

MEMPHIS, TENNESSEE: UNION STATION (1913)

Union Station was built originally to serve five railroads in 1913. In the Italian Renaissance style, it was built of Vermont granite and midwest limestone and measured 285 feet by 84 feet. The architect was John A. Galvin. This photograph was taken about 1940.

In 1966 three railroads were still using the station, but abandoned it due to lack of business. After some legal maneuvers when the city claimed abandonment was illegal, it was partially reopened. On February 27, 1968, however, the Louisville & Nashville ran its last train into Memphis, and the Southern, then the only other occupant, removed its last service shortly thereafter. Present plans call for razing and possible construction of a Post Office on the site. *L. & N.*

MILWAUKEE, WISCONSIN: OLD UNION DEPOT   Chicago, Milwaukee & St. Paul

"Old Union Depot" at the foot of Reed Street is pictured in these two photographs from the 1870s. It was from here that the first Milwaukee to Chicago passenger train ran in 1873. The station served the Milwaukee & Prairie du Chien Railroad, which was succeeded by the Milwaukee & St. Paul Railway in 1868, and also the Wisconsin Central Railroad, later the Soo Line.   *C. M. St. P. & P.*

This depot was undoubtedly a busy place as the horse cars, hotel omnibuses, carriages, and wagons indicate. It was abandoned December 25, 1886, when the new Union Station on Everett Street was opened. *Milwaukee Road.*

MILWAUKEE, WISCONSIN: UNION STATION (1886) Chicago, Milwaukee & St. Paul

For eighty years this Union Station was one of Milwaukee's famous landmarks. Opened in 1886, modern Gothic in style, it was the pride of the Milwaukee Road. A few words of contemporary description are appropriate: "... main entrance is formed of a triple arch supported by columns of polished granite. It is reached by a flight of easy steps. The swinging doors of polished oak are a few feet inside the arch, being surmounted by stained glass windows in beautiful designs. These admit the visitor into a large central hall which bisects the building. . . ." The car sheds were 600 feet long and 100 feet wide, covering five tracks. A new station at the intersection of Fifth Street and West St. Paul Avenue replaced this venerable building on August 4, 1965.   *Milwaukee Road.*

Locomotive No. 732, built in the early 1900s, might have been seen at Milwaukee Union Station.

MILWAUKEE, WISCONSIN (1889)   Chicago & North Western

The Chicago & North Western's terminal depot in Milwaukee was designed by
architect Charles S. Trost and built in 1889. It was an L-shaped side station of
stone and brick with a 176-foot tower. Its train shed covered four tracks and was
440 feet long.

The "W. W. Greene," engine No. 600, was a 4-4-0 locomotive.

R. G. Woods Collection.

MONTREAL, QUEBEC, CANADA (1887)   Canadian National

This is old Bonaventure Station built originally by the Grand Trunk in 1887.
When opened, it was the ultimate in elegance and comfort. Destroyed by fire in
1916, it was rebuilt without the towers, and it served the Grand Trunk, later the
Canadian National, until 1943 when the present Central Station was opened. *C. N.*

The old Bonaventure Station waiting room shows the handsome styling of a bygone era. From the patterned floor to the wall and entrance carvings, the decor was richly ornamental.
C. N.

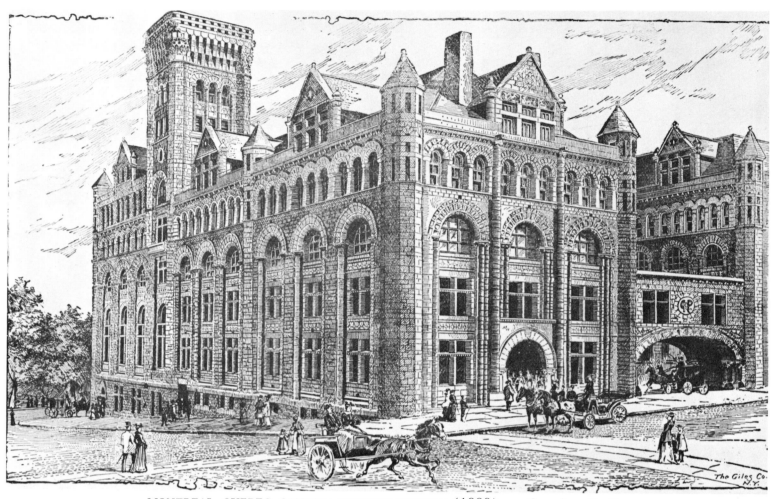

MONTREAL, QUEBEC, CANADA: WINDSOR STATION (1888)   Canadian Pacific

Windsor Station was designed by architect Bruce Price for the Canadian Pacific and completed in 1888 at a cost of $250,000. This old drawing shows its original appearance. Built of stone, it was four stories high and covered an area of 204 feet by 70 feet.

The 2-6-0 type engine, No. 3011, might have traveled to Windsor Station.

In 1911 and 1912, a large addition was built dwarfing the original building (far right). In 1954 the accounting wing (on the left) was erected. *C. P.*

No. 3100, a large 4-8-4 locomotive, was photographed in 1929.

NASHVILLE, TENNESSEE Louisville & Nashville

Church Street, Nashville's first railroad depot, was built by the Nashville & Chattanooga Railroad prior to 1854, when the line was completed between those cities. Later the Louisville & Nashville and the Nashville & Northwestern railroads used this station. The area served as a base for the U.S. Military Railroads during the Civil War, and the photograph was taken during this period. Some sixteen locomotives are in the picture, and the cars at the left were forerunners of the familiar caboose.

This is Church Street Station as it appeared in 1895 after it was remodeled and dressed up for the Tennessee Centennial Exposition. Five years later it was demolished when a new Union Station was built farther south. *L. & N.*

NEW HAVEN, CONNECTICUT (1848-1849)   New Haven

Henry Austin was the architect who designed this early New Haven station, which was built in 1848 and 1849. A combination of several styles in one building, it was, however, the first with a campanile. Carroll Meeks described the depot: "There was a shed, a bridge over a cut, and stairs down to narrow platforms. Although the street-level building with towers and pergolas was carefully studied and highly original, the operating parts, cramped and airless, were so inadequate that it was remodeled twice during its first two years. . . . While the plan was almost perfectly symmetrical, the elevation was not. Fantasy began above the cornice. Austin placed a campanile at one end, a truncated pagoda over the main entrance, and at the far left an anomalous feature which synthesizes elements from the other two. To the conventional round-headed arches and brackets of the Italian Villa style, he added Indian and Chinese motive."

Locomotive No. 9, a 4-4-0 engine, was typical of those that stopped at New Haven in the 1870s.

New Haven's station in the 1870s and 1880s is pictured by A. E. Bishop, the photographer who was famous for his early locomotive action pictures. In this photograph, the open-sided observation car is also of interest as is the overhead bridge seen in the background, which was the means for coaling the engines.

NEW ORLEANS, LOUISIANA   Louisville & Nashville

This drawing shows the second station in New Orleans, built in the 1870s, as it appeared about twenty years later. It replaced the first, on the same site, which had been built by the New Orleans, Mobile & Texas Railroad which the L. & N. acquired in 1880. Jefferson Davis's funeral train left here for Richmond on May 28, 1893.   L. & N.

NEW ORLEANS, LOUISIANA (1906)   Louisville & Nashville

Here is the engineer's perspective drawing for the new station proposed to replace the old building of the 1870s. This was completed in 1906 and opened with great fanfare. A portion of the film *A Streetcar Named Desire* was made in the area using an L. & N. steam locomotive. Thousands of commuters who worked in New Orleans but lived in smaller nearby towns along the Gulf coast passed through this station. It closed in 1954 when a new New Orleans Union passenger terminal opened, and was sold in 1956. In 1958 it was demolished.   L. & N.

NEW YORK, NEW YORK: GRAND CENTRAL (1871)   New York Central

On November 15, 1869, under the direction of Isaac C. Buckhout and Commodore Vanderbilt's son William, work was begun on what was to be the country's largest terminal. Construction progressed rapidly and in just under two years it was completed. The station faced 42nd Street for 249 feet and extended nearly 700 feet north. It was fireproof, built of iron, granite, glass, and brick with cement and concrete used instead of mortar. All ornamental cast iron was painted white. Three towers faced 42nd Street and upon each was inscribed the name of one of the three railroads using the terminal.

The train shed was designed by Joseph Duclos or R. G. Hatfield, both employed by the Architectural Iron Works, the builders. It was 695 feet long and 200 feet wide spanning twelve tracks.

The New York & Harlem was the first railroad to use the new station starting October 18, 1871, but little note was made of it in the newspapers of that day for the great Chicago fire commandeered all space. The New York Central began using the station a few weeks later, but the New York & New Haven did not use the facilities until the spring of 1872, when its 27th Street and Park Avenue station (where the first Madison Square Garden was to rise) was abandoned. >

Each of the three railroads had its own waiting room, ticket offices, baggage handling, and other facilities, and there was no connection between them until 1898 when modernization was undertaken and facilities common to all were provided. This rebuilding was planned by Bradford L. Gilbert, and additional stories heightened the building which might be termed the Second Grand Central.

For years after its opening, Grand Central was the showplace of New York, and for a long time it ranked next to the Capitol in Washington in national esteem. The rebuilding in the 1890s was hardly finished when, within five years, the third and greatest station was being planned to replace it.

DISPATCHER'S ROOM
"OPENING A DOOR"
BY SIGNAL

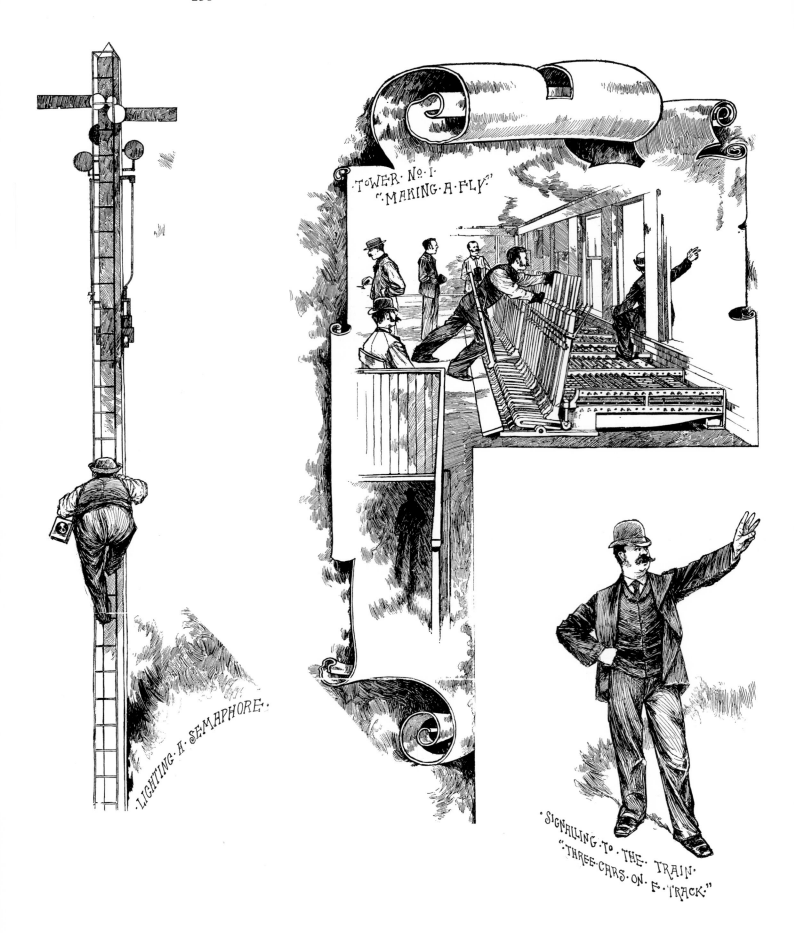

LIGHTING·A·SEMAPHORE·

TOWER·N̲O̲·1·
":MAKING·A·FLY"

·SIGNALLING·TO·THE·TRAIN·
"·THREE·CARS·ON·F·TRACK·"

THE·DISPATCHER'S·HOUSE

Chas Bunnell

·YARDMAN·
·TALKING·WITH·A·TOWER·

AN·OILER·
·GOING·THE·ROUNDS·

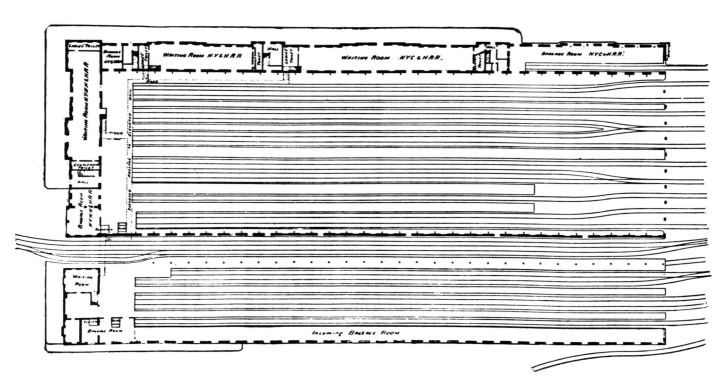

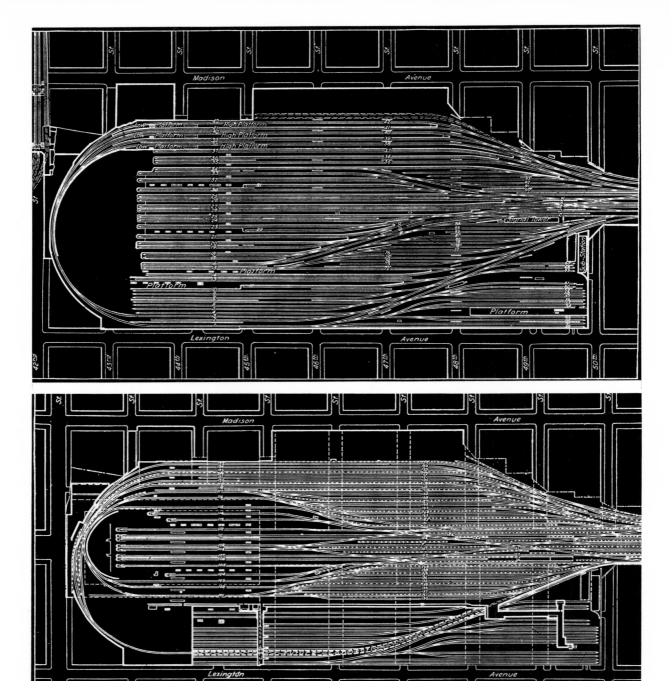

NEW YORK, NEW YORK: THIRD GRAND CENTRAL (1913)   New York Central

Electricity was the key word behind the planning for the new Grand Central. To power the train operations in the Park Avenue tunnel and station area and eliminate the smoke, it had become a necessity. William J. Wilgus, Chief Engineer of the New York Central, was the man in charge of the planning, and he was responsible for the ingenious design of a two-track-level station—the first of its kind. Based upon the track layout, top architects were asked to submit plans for the building proper. Charles Reed and Allen Stem of St. Paul were chosen, and June 1903 marked the beginning of the great project.

The demolition of the old station was started in August, but it remained partly in use until June 1910. Meanwhile, the excavation for the two track levels proceeded. A million cubic yards of earth and two million cubic yards of granite had to be blasted and removed, opening an area 40 feet deep, 770 feet wide, and half a mile long. Temporary station facilities had, of course, to be provided, and all operations had to go forward with a minimum of interference to scheduled train operations. By 1907 all trains were being powered electrically.

There were difficulties with the designers, and other architects. Warren and Wetmore entered the picture, but Reed was the guiding light. Eventually it was finished, and the great new Grand Central Station was opened February 2, 1913. It has been said, "No better station of its size has ever been built," and the main concourse is "one of the finest interior spaces ever erected."

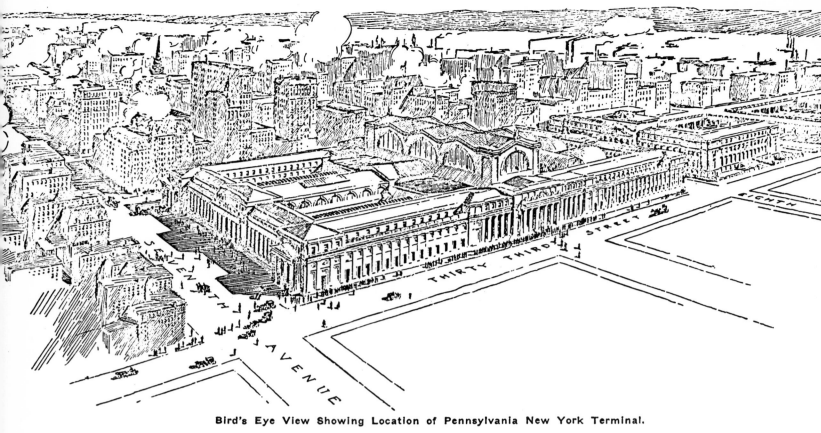

Bird's Eye View Showing Location of Pennsylvania New York Terminal.

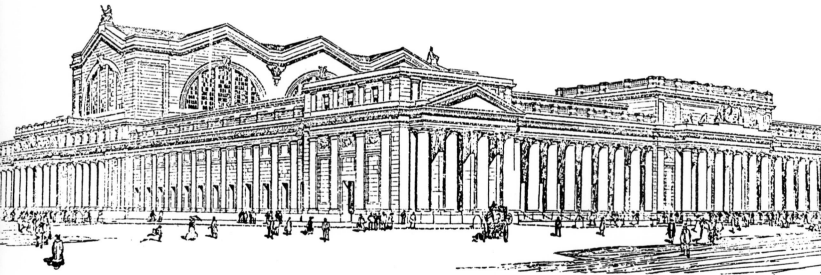

General Elevation of Station.

NEW YORK, NEW YORK: PENNSYLVANIA STATION (1910) Pennsylvania Railroad

The need for a direct entrance into Manhattan had been evident to Pennsylvania Railroad officials for many years, and much thought and planning were devoted to how this might be done. The final and present line evolved from one of five plans, and after franchises and preliminaries had been worked out, work on the tunnels under the Hudson and East rivers was commenced on June 10, 1903. McKim, Mead & White were the architects for the monumental station which extended a city block, 430 feet, on Seventh Avenue between 32nd and 33rd streets. Three million cubic yards of excavation were removed, and 27,000 tons of steel, 1,140 carloads of granite, and 15,000,000 bricks went into the building, which was started in June 1908. Its general waiting room, one of the largest such spaces in the world, was 277 feet long, 107 feet wide, and 150 feet high. The train concourse was 341 feet by 277 feet, and incoming and outgoing passengers were accommodated on two separate levels.

The entire station area covered twenty-eight acres. The tunnels were completed in 1906, and the sixteen miles of track installed included twenty-one standing tracks, eight of which were to be used by the Long Island Railroad. The trackage provides

>

General Waiting Room, Pennsylvania Station.

storage space for 386 passenger cars. When completed the total cost approached $14 million. The Long Island started using the station on September 8, 1910, and on November 27 of that year it was in full operation.

Described as the greatest side station ever built, Penn Station was an outstanding landmark, and the building's removal through the 1960s has been much regretted by many people besides historians. Its services still remain, of course, but "Penn Station, New York" as called out by trainmen is just another station stop today.

Pennsylvania Railroad.

PASADENA, CALIFORNIA (1886)   Atchison, Topeka & Santa Fe

The Raymond Station was built by the Los Angeles & San Gabriel Valley Railroad in 1886, when they constructed the railroad from Los Angeles to the San
Gabriel River, and this was the first station in Pasadena. It was located one mile
west of the present building which dates from 1895. The Santa Fe System acquired
the L. A. & S. G. V. in 1887.   *A. T. S. F.*

PHILADELPHIA, PENNSYLVANIA: BROAD STREET STATION (1881)

Pennsylvania Railroad

The Pennsylvania Railroad's main station in Philadelphia was originally in
West Philadelphia at 32nd and Market streets, built in time to handle the crowds
which came to the Centennial Exhibition. Soon after that it was decided that a
new passenger terminal nearer the center of the city was necessary, and plans were

made accordingly. This entailed an elevated line avoiding street crossings at grade to bring the tracks almost to Broad Street. The new passenger station was a four-story building of Gothic design across from City Hall, and it opened for business on December 5, 1881. It had nine tracks under a double train shed, and according to early timetables, 160 trains used it daily, including those of the Philadelphia, Wilmington & Baltimore.

In only a few more years enlarging became necessary, and Frank Furness was the architect who planned the work. A large office building in conjunction with the station was built south of the original structure, and in 1891 the famous Broad Street Station was opened. The tracks were increased to twelve, and then sixteen, and the largest train shed ever built—300 feet wide, 595 feet long, and 108 feet high—was installed over the two older sheds which were then removed.

By 1910, 578 trains daily used Broad Street Station and it had become renowned not only for its trains, but for its decor and service to travelers. The main waiting room on the second, or train, floor had an open fireplace; its Grand Staircase

>

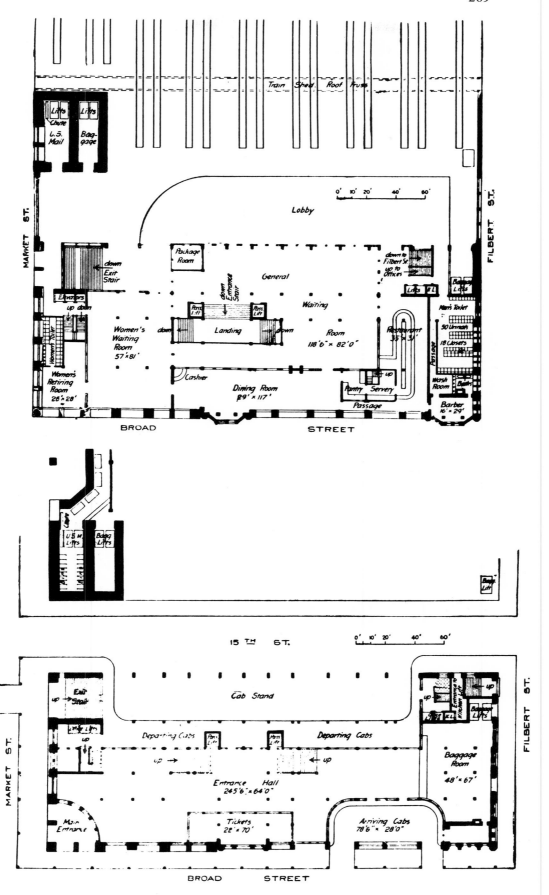

from street level to this floor was of solid marble with ornamental railings. Externally and internally, plaques, panels, and other bas reliefs embellished the building. The most massive plaque, Karl Biter's "The Spirit of Transportation," was removed and installed in the new 30th Street Station in 1933.

The station restaurant, the Savarin (although under Union News management in later years) was considered the finest in the city with a 120-table dining room and 76-seat marble lunch counter. Practically all the famous people who came to Philadelphia dined here as well, of course, as many local folk who were faithful patrons.

The end came for old Broad Street Station at 9:57 P.M. on April 26, 1952, when, after seventy years of service, the last train left the terminal, some three thousand people being on hand to see it go. The Philadelphia Orchestra with Eugene Ormandy, top railroad officials, the Mayor, and city dignitaries were there, and as the train pulled out, "Auld Lang Syne" was sung by all.

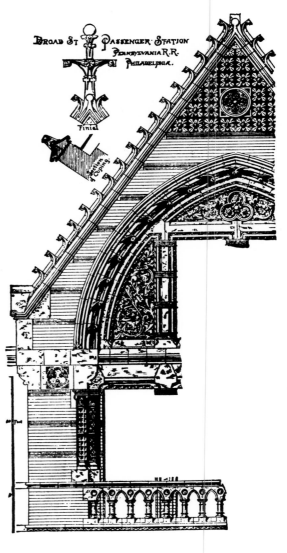

BROAD ST PASSENGER STATION
PENNSYLVANIA R.R.
PHILADELPHIA.

Finial

PHILADELPHIA, PENNSYLVANIA: READING TERMINAL (1893)   Reading

In the same year that Broad Street Station opened, work was begun on the Reading's new station. Architect F. H. Kimball was responsible for the design, and Wilson Brothers and Company, civil engineers and architects, collaborated and were in charge of construction. The first illustration is from one of their drawings of the original design, although an additional story was added. The exterior was designed in the Italian Renaissance style, and a contemporary accolade sums up opinion thus: "The Philadelphia & Reading Railroad Company has succeeded in erecting one of the handsomest terminal passenger stations in the world, so that due credit should be given to the railroad company and to the designers for an achievement that any American can be justly proud of."

Originally the main lobby and ticket offices were on the first, or street, floor but since 1948 all passenger facilities have been combined with the main waiting room of the second, or train, floor. An excellent restaurant used to be located on this level, and its cuisine was justly famous.

Besides the building proper, the train shed is especially noteworthy for it was one of the largest built in this country, one of the last built, and it is still in service. It is 559 feet long, 256 feet wide, and 90 feet high at its maximum, covering thirteen tracks and their platforms. Under it from its earliest days has been Reading Terminal Market, still a mecca for gourmets, where delicacies, seafood, fine meats, and produce brought from Pennsylvania Dutch country farms can be found.

The 1896 Philadelphia and New York express, pulled by locomotive No. 378—a 4-2-2 Baldwin engine—was photographed leaving Reading Terminal.

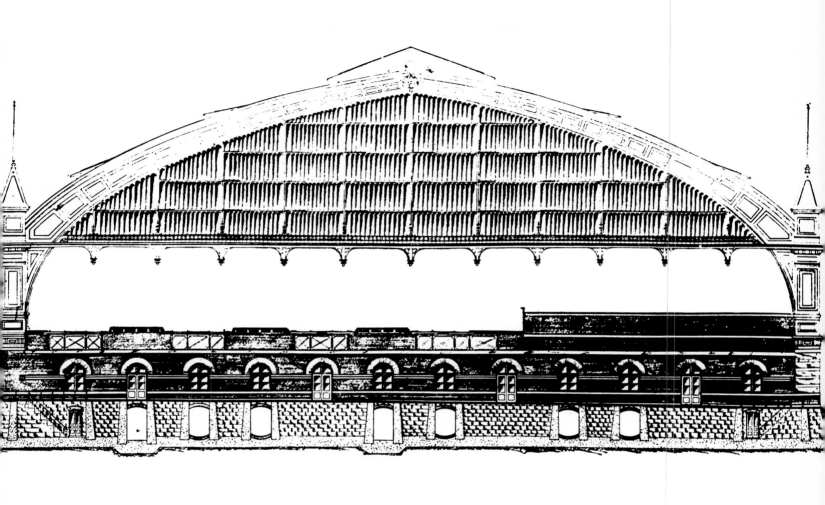

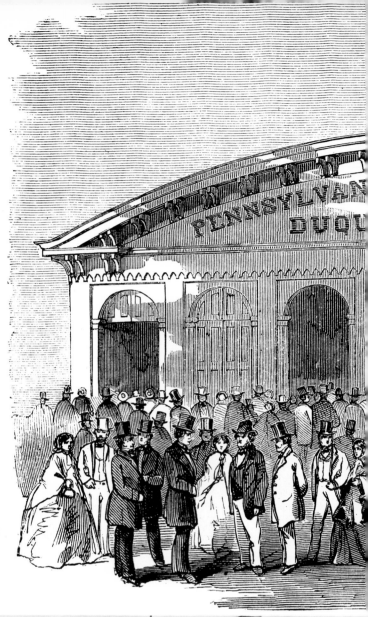

PITTSBURGH, PENNSYLVANIA: UNION STATION   Pennsylvania Railroad

Pittsburgh's first Union Station on the site of Fort Duquesne, north of Liberty Street at Grant Street, was built in the 1850s. The second was a little farther east, a large four-story building completed in 1865. Twelve years later it was destroyed by fire during the riots of 1877.

>

A smaller station was built on the same site and served until it was replaced in 1902 by a new combined terminal and twelve-story office building. Daniel Burnham was the architect, and to improve the approach to the station, he designed a great arched vestibule or carriage concourse for the entrance to the main building.

The train shed was the last of the great single-span arched type, and the third erected by the Pennsylvania. It was 550 feet in length, 240 feet wide, and 110 feet high. It stood until 1947.

PITTSBURGH, PENNSYLVANIA   Baltimore & Ohio
This is the Baltimore & Ohio's Pittsburgh station as it appeared about 1915.

PROVIDENCE, RHODE ISLAND (1848)   New Haven

The Union Depot at Providence was the first major American railroad station to be designed by Thomas Tefft, who was but twenty-two years old at the time. It was also the first in the new Romanesque manner. "As late as 1885 it was voted one of the twenty best buildings in the U.S. . . . a rare distinction for any depot, especially one thirty-seven years old" (Carroll Meeks). The picture shows the second Rhode Island Regiment leaving for the front in 1861.   *N. H.*

PROVIDENCE, RHODE ISLAND (1899)   New Haven

The second Providence Union Station was opened in 1899, and until recently had a train shed, its most distinguishing feature. It was built across a new thoroughfare, Francis Street, and ramps connected the street to the platforms. It is interesting to note that the City of Providence, through injunction suits, held up the use of the new station for two years and compelled the installation of the train shed which was only recently removed. In the picture, the building in the background is, of course, Rhode Island's state capitol.

RICHMOND, VIRGINIA   Chesapeake & Ohio

Of about 1900 vintage, the architecture of the C. & O.'s Richmond station is quite interesting. If it were not for the modern signal in the picture, the photograph would seem to be decades older than the 1960s when it was made.   *C. & O.*

ST. LOUIS, MISSOURI (1875)   Missouri Pacific

The first station in St. Louis was this building of 1875. The Pullman Palace Car
Company had offices there as the sign indicates.

ST. LOUIS, MISSOURI: UNION STATION (1891-94)

Theodore C. Link and Edward B. Cameron were the architects of St. Louis's Romanesque Union Station. It was, briefly, the largest depot in the world and served twenty-seven railroads. Owned by the Terminal Railroad Association of St. Louis, the station area covers 13¼ acres, the building is 606 feet long and 80 feet wide, and the train shed is 630 feet long and 600 feet wide with five spans covering thirty-two tracks. The shed was designed by George H. Pegram and has a capacity of 330 80-foot passenger cars. It was said that the Grand Hall was its best feature, and externally it was effectively picturesque. ➤

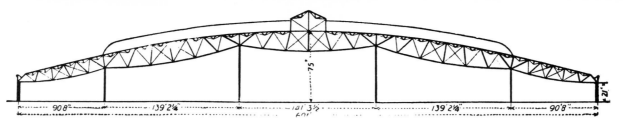

FIG. 651.—PERSPECTIVE OF EXTERIOR OF TRAIN-SHED.

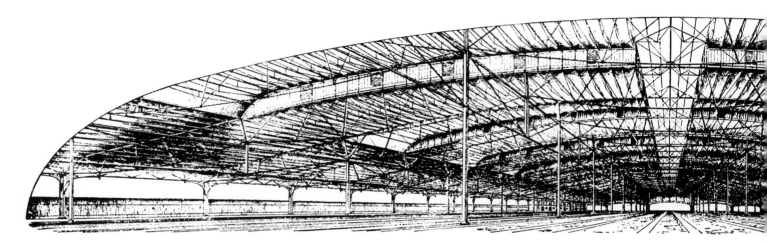

FIG. 652.—PERSPECTIVE OF INTERIOR OF TRAIN-SHED.

Missouri Pacific engine No. 5306, a 4-8-4 locomotive, was photographed leaving Union Station in 1929.

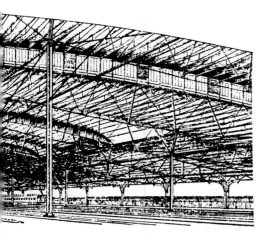

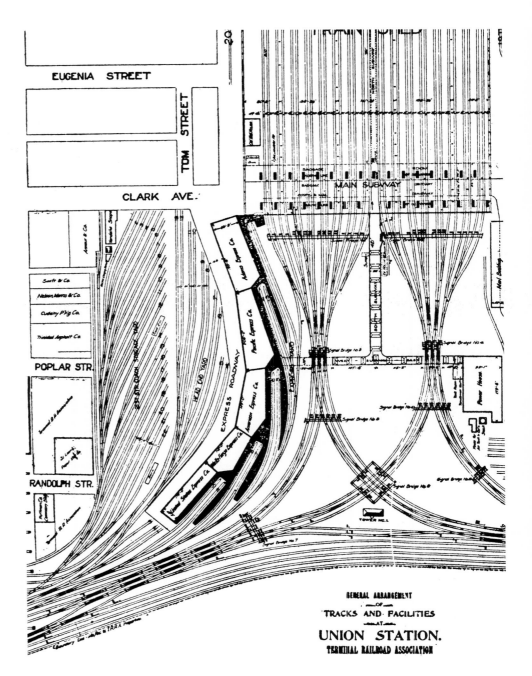

EUGENIA STREET

TOM STREET

CLARK AVE.

POPLAR STR.

RANDOLPH STR.

MAIN SUBWAY

GENERAL ARRANGEMENT
— OF —
TRACKS AND FACILITIES
— AT —
UNION STATION.
TERMINAL RAILROAD ASSOCIATION

SALT LAKE CITY, UTAH (1909)   Denver & Rio Grande

Here is the Salt Lake City station of the D. & R. G. as it appeared in 1909, the year it was completed. The photographs show the street side with waiting hacks and conveyances, and the interior of the waiting room.

The view at the track side of the building was taken a few years later with a waiting train and engine 802.   *Library, State Historical Society of Colorado.*

SEATTLE, WASHINGTON (1906)   Great Northern

 Seattle's King Street Station was completed May 9, 1906, and was then described as unequaled by any city of the same size in the United States. Its tall tower was, and is still, a landmark. The Northern Pacific and Great Northern jointly operate this station.

SEATTLE, WASHINGTON (1910)   Union Pacific

When built in 1910, this was called the Oregon-Washington station of the Oregon Railroad & Navigation Company, later Union Pacific, which jointly used it with the Chicago, Milwaukee & St. Paul. The photograph is from the 1950s, and the tower of King Street Station can be seen in the right background.

WASHINGTON, D.C. (1851)   Baltimore & Ohio

This is the old B. & O. station, built in Washington in 1851, as it appeared in the 1880s after the wing at the right had been added. It was at Pennsylvania Avenue and 2nd Street and was built in the Italian Villa style. Abraham Lincoln arrived here for his inauguration as President on February 23, 1861.

Another view of the B. & O. station taken about 1900 shows a local passenger train and part of the train shed.

WASHINGTON, D.C. (1873)   Pennsylvania Railroad

The Baltimore & Potomac terminal was designed by Joseph M. Wilson, the engineer and architect who planned many of the Pennsylvania's projects, and was built at 6th and B streets, the site of the present Union Station. Finished in 1873, it has been described as "exceedingly handsome, the whole building finished in first class style—and heated by steam throughout."

It was in the waiting room here that James A. Garfield, twentieth President of the United States, was shot on July 2, 1881. He died from the wound at his home in Elberon, New Jersey, on September 19. To mark the spot where the President fell, a star was placed in the floor, and on the wall opposite, a marble tablet. This station was replaced by the present Union Station in 1907.

‹

WASHINGTON, D.C.: UNION STATION (1907)   Pennsylvania Railroad
Baltimore & Ohio

The site for Washington's Union Station was selected by a committee consisting of D. H. Burnham, C. F. McKim, Augustus St. Gaudens, and Frederick Law Olmstead, Jr., which had been appointed to prepare a general plan for the beautifying and development of the city and its parks. The building was designed by Daniel H. Burnham and was completed in 1907. It is the property of the Washington Terminal Company whose stock is equally owned by the Pennsylvania and the Baltimore & Ohio.

It has been called "the perfect example of the city gate designed in perfect harmony with the architecture of the community for which it serves as an entrance," classical but not a facsimile of any classic building.

The building is 663 feet long and 211 feet wide, of white marble and granite. Its waiting room is 220 feet long and 130 feet wide, with a Roman barrel-vaulted roof 93 feet high in the center. The concourse, said to be the largest room used for any purpose in the world, is 760 feet long and 130 feet wide. There are thirty-three tracks: twenty stub tracks at street or concourse level, and thirteen through tracks for trains to and from the south.

An event occurred on the morning of January 15, 1953, at Washington Union Station, which will be remembered longer by its staff than the most important VIP who ever passed through there.

The Federal Express, train No. 173, had left Boston at eleven the previous evening and had brake trouble west of Providence, losing fifty-six minutes. It made up time between New Haven and New York, leaving there eight minutes late. The brakes were in use about thirty times between New York and Baltimore without any difficulties.

Approaching Washington Terminal, engineer Harry Brower tried a brake application as he neared Tower C two miles away, but with no result; then an emergency brake, but there was no air. He realized that the Federal was a runaway and about all he could do was sound the horn. The conductor and trainmen in different cars could tell from the speed and the horn that the train was out of control. The towerman at Tower C had already lined up the switches for the terminal track and there was no time to make any changes; he called the next tower, K, and the operator there called the stationmaster. The man on duty knew that the train was due on track 16 and by then could see it coming. He yelled a general warning and alerted the people on the concourse.

The train came through the concourse fence, wrecked the stationmaster's office, and then the 230-ton, GG-1 engine went through the concourse floor pulling two cars along into the basement baggage room. Miraculously no one was killed, although a number of people were hurt.

Because of the expected crowds of visitors due only five days away for Dwight D. Eisenhower's inauguration, the concourse was temporarily planked over the locomotive, which was removed within the next two weeks. The cost in property damage was close to a million dollars.   ›

PART V

The Stations That Were

*T*HESE ARE THE STATIONS WHICH HAVE BEGUN A NEW LEASE ON LIFE—GIVEN A second chance instead of being demolished by the wrecker.

Many, many more than the few examples illustrated are being saved and converted to useful purposes. Basically, whether any of these historic old buildings can survive depends upon location, and whether a business, civic, or educational use is contemplated in the area. If not in the "right" one, that is the end; rather than pay taxes on a building no longer useful, the railroad eliminates it.

Historic is the right word for this category of Americana—a type of architecture unique in purpose. Whatever enterprise the former station is used for, its background is unmistakably there and in the minds of visitors or patrons.

BALTIMORE, MARYLAND: MOUNT CLARE (1831)   Baltimore & Ohio

Mount Clare has been awarded a far better fate than most old railroad stations. To become a museum and especially a railroad museum, was the ultimate for this historic building. In it and the adjoining old roundhouse are preserved some of the finest and rarest railroad relics extant. There are small objects such as lanterns, bells, and headlights, paintings (particularly those of Herbert D. Stitt), memorabilia in frames, and models including two different operating miniature layouts. In the roundhouse are historic locomotives and cars dating back to the earliest days of the B. & O. Seeing this collection is a must for any visitor to Baltimore. *B. & O.*

Locomotive No. 43, an 0-8-0 type engine, was built at the Mount Clare shops in 1854.

BETHLEHEM, PENNSYLVANIA (1873)   Central Railroad of New Jersey

This Bethlehem station was built in 1873 and today looks even better than in this photograph taken in the 1930s.

In 1962, in cooperation with the "Historic Bethlehem" project, the Junior Chamber of Commerce started a restoration of this building which is now nearing completion. The original estimated cost was $17,500, but so far about $40,000 has actually been spent to preserve this former Central Railroad of New Jersey station. The exterior has been retained in its original form, but the interior was completely modernized including a large meeting room on the second floor where living quarters once were. Offices are on the first floor. The Jaycees deserve much commendation for this historic preservation project.   ➤

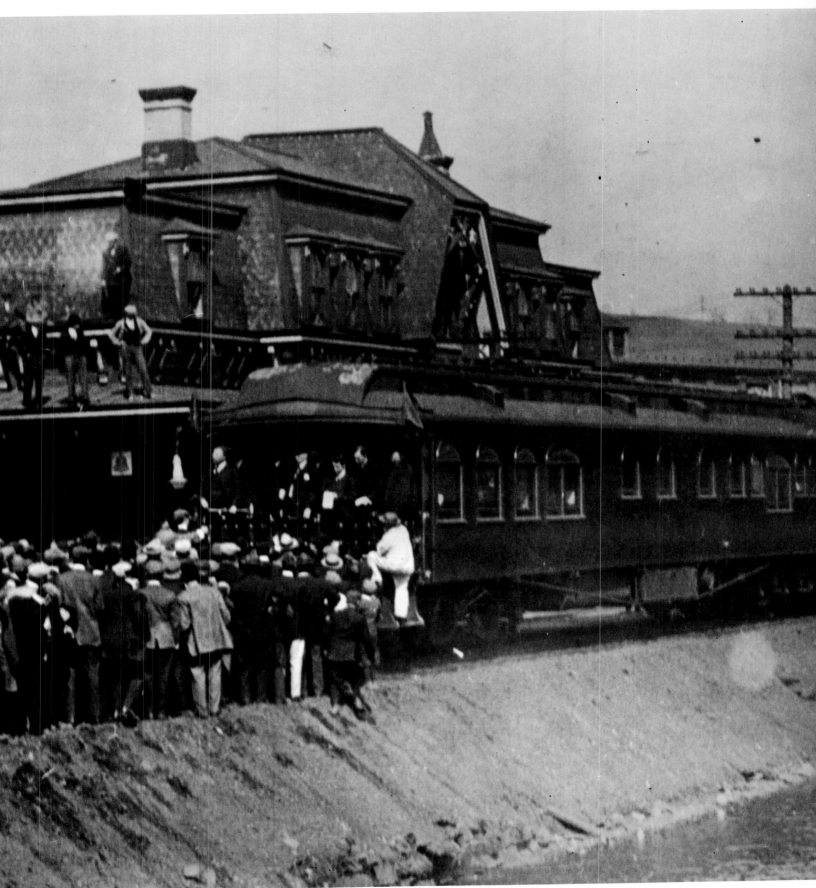

A famous personage who visited this Bethlehem station was Teddy Roosevelt,
shown here making a rear platform speech during his 1912 campaign.

BRIARCLIFF MANOR, NEW YORK   New York Central

On the Putnam Division about thirty miles from New York is the Briarcliff Manor station, shown in these photographs of the 1900s. The building is now a library.

BRYN ATHYN, PENNSYLVANIA   Reading

Bryn Athyn is on the single-track Newtown Branch of the Reading fifteen miles from Reading Terminal. Commuting trains still stop here, but the post office sign is unmistakable.

CHATHAM, MASSACHUSETTS   New Haven

Originally on the Chatham Railroad, later incorporated into the New Haven, these pictures show Chatham station as it was in the 1900s and as it is today. The restoration was done by the town of Chatham and the building is used as a railroad museum.   *Thomas Annin.*

No. 31, a 2-6-0 Hinkley engine built in 1872, was photographed with its crew about 1896.

EMINENCE, KENTUCKY   Louisville & Nashville

No passenger service is available at Eminence anymore. The station dates from the 1920s, and the only trains stopping are occasional freights. The town library now occupies the building.

Typical of the locomotives that stopped at Eminence during its railroad days is No. 330, a 4-6-2 engine.

GETTYSBURG, PENNSYLVANIA (1850s)   Western Maryland

Before Lincoln came to Gettysburg to make his famous address, this old station was there. Today it houses the Tourist Information Office.   *W. R. Hicks.*

A full-size replica about a mile south on Route 15 contains the Lincoln Train Museum with a simulated train ride of Lincoln's trip to Gettysburg and a collection of railroadiana, models, and toy trains formerly at the Alexander Museum in Yardley, Pennsylvania.   *Lincoln Train Museum.*

LIMESTONE SPRINGS, KENTUCKY Louisville & Nashville

Regular passenger service to Limestone Springs on the L. & N.'s Springfield Branch ceased in 1953. The station is now owned by Schenley Distillers which have offices in the Swiss-chalet-type building. *L. & N.*

NORTH BRANCH, NEW JERSEY Central Railroad of New Jersey

Commuting trains still stop at North Branch station, but the post office now conducts the main business.

PELHAM MANOR, NEW YORK

New Haven

On the Harlem River Branch about twelve miles from the terminal in the Bronx was perhaps the most elaborate and finest suburban station the New Haven ever had. It was reputed to have cost $125,000 in the early 1900s and was solidly built of stone. Because the Harlem River terminal was so far uptown in New York, it never attracted enough commuters, and service was suspended in the 1930s.

In the 1930s the Westchester Model Club negotiated a lease with the New Haven for $1.00 yearly, and one of the best club model railroads was built in this station. It was a well-known installation for years until the land and building were sold. Today cars travel on the New England Expressway over this spot although the tracks alongside remain.

A small part of the extensive O-gauge track layout is shown below.

PHILADELPHIA, PENNSYLVANIA: GRAVERS (1888)   Reading

Gravers on the Reading's Chestnut Hill Branch is shown in this photograph taken shortly after its opening. The branch was later double-tracked. The building is presently rented and used as a dwelling.

PITTSBURGH, PENNSYLVANIA: NORTHSIDE   Pennsylvania

Across the Allegheny River from Pittsburgh's main station, on the P. Ft. W. & C. line is Northside station. The waiting room, closed since 1935, was leased by Studebaker dealer Chester A. Reed for a showroom. As the picture taken in the 1940s shows, it served this purpose well.   *Fred McLeod.*
                                                                Studebaker.

>

No. 8278 was photographed on a zero-degree morning in 1932, west bound from Pittsburgh on the Fort Wayne Division.

SHELBURNE, VERMONT Rutland

This is the old Rutland Railroad's Shelburne Depot which was moved a few hundred feet to the grounds of the Shelburne Museum. A Central Vermont ten-wheeler and several passenger and freight cars are on the station track.

SOUTH WALLINGFORD, VERMONT   Rutland

This Rutland Railroad station was moved from South Wallingford to Pawlet and has become a year-round restaurant there. Comparing pictures, the fine restoration was made just in time. The "before" photograph was made in 1961.

Thomas Annin.

317

WATERBURY, CONNECTICUT (1909)   New Haven

The Waterbury station was built to the design of architects McKim, Mead and White in 1909 and boasted one of the highest, as well as the last clock tower built for twenty-five years. It is now occupied by the newspaper offices of the *Waterbury Republican-American.*   *N. H.*

BIBLIOGRAPHY

Twelve authors. *The American Railway*. New York: Charles Scribner & Sons, 1889.

Berg, Walter G. *Buildings and Structures of American Railroads*. New York: John Wiley & Sons, 1892.

Delaware & Hudson Railway Stations. Albany, N.Y.: Delaware & Hudson, 1928.

Droege, John A. *Passenger Terminals and Trains*. New York: McGraw Hill, 1916.

Hungerford, Edward. *The History of the Baltimore & Ohio*. New York: G. P. Putnam's Sons, 1928.

————. *Men and Iron*. New York: Thomas Y. Crowell, 1938.

Meeks, Carroll. *The Railroad Station*. New Haven, Yale University Press, 1960.

Wilson, William Bender. *History of the Pennsylvania Railroad*. Philadelphia: Henry T. Coates, 1895.

INDEX